P9-BXZ-467

DATE			

Frances Tenenbaum, Series Editor

HOUGHTON MIFFLIN COMPANY
Boston • New York   1999

Fragrant Gardens

How to select and make the most of scented flowers and leaves

PETER LOEWER

For information about permission to reproduce selections from this book,
write to Permissions, Houghton Mifflin Company, 215 Park Avenue South,
New York, New York 10003.

Taylor's Guide and *Taylor's Weekend Gardening Guides* are registered trademarks of
Houghton Mifflin Company.

Library of Congress Cataloging-in-Publication Data

Loewer, H. Peter.
    Fragrant gardens : how to select and make the most of scented flowers and
leaves / Peter Loewer.
        p.   cm. — (Taylor's weekend gardening guides)
    Includes index.
    ISBN 0-395-88492-6
    1. Fragrant gardens. 2. Aromatic plants. I. Title. II. Series.
SB454.3.F7L65 1999
635.9'68 — dc21   98–38756

Printed in the United States of America

WCT 10 9 8 7 6 5 4 3 2 1

Book design by Deborah Fillion
Cover photograph © by Derek Fell

CONTENTS

In the late 1500s, Christopher Marlowe wrote the following lines for his poem "The Passionate Shepherd to His Love":

"And I will make thee beds of roses
And a thousand fragrant posies."

In 1860, some 270 years later, Ralph Waldo Emerson opined in *The Conduct of Life,* "I wish that life should not be cheap, but sacred. I wish the days to be as centuries, loaded, fragrant."

The first is a declaration of love, the second a philosophy of life. Both reflect on one of mankind's five primary senses — the sense of smell.

Many idiomatic sayings are also associated with this sense, including a few that are not complimentary, for example, "It smells to high heaven"; "I am beginning to smell a rat"; and "They wrinkled their noses at the smell." For every ill smell that's recalled, however, there are dozens of proverbs, axioms, and, yes, even clichés, linked to pleasant memories that usually involve flowers.

Trey Fromme, a young landscape architect lecturing at Longwood Gardens, once talked about the fragrant garden and said that we don't often use "odor or fragrance as a focal point in the garden." It's time to do so in the garden world.

I hope that this small book helps to point the way.

———————————

*The perennial daturas (*Brugmansia × insignis *'Pink') produces beautiful pendent flowers when summer heats up.*

CHAPTER 1

ABOUT FRAGRANCES

In May of 1978 I had the opportunity to interview Nigel Nicholson at Sissinghurst Castle. After a tour of his mother's garden we went to the living room for tea, where on a table piled with books (and an overflowing ashtray) sat a large glass bowl filled with white tree peonies *(Paeonia suffruticosa)*. To this day when I smell the clean, light fragrance of our own newly opened tree peonies, I instantly recall that early afternoon, the sweet pungence of the blackberry tea, and the murmurings of the nearby visitors wandering the gardens of the castle.

Fragrances reach across the decades like physical links to the past, reminding us of times long forgotten. A floral scent will trigger the memory: the faint odor of orange that recalls the mock orangebush that grew by my grandmother's front porch; the sweet but cloying scent of tuberoses that my Aunt Ida would force into bloom for Thanksgiving dinner; and the light and citric smell of the evening primroses that bloom every year in my own garden, as they open their sulfur yellow flowers to the darkening skies of evening.

"A garden full of sweet odours is a garden full of charm," wrote Louise Beebe Wilder in *The Fragrant Garden*.

> A most precious kind of charm not to be implanted by mere skill
> in horticulture or power of purse, and which is beyond explain-

The windmill jasmine (Jasminum nitidum)
originally came from the Admiralty Islands,
and its fragrance is starry sweet.

ing. It is born of sensitive and very personal preferences yet its appeal is almost universal. Fragrance speaks to many to whom color and form say little, and it can bring as irresistibly as music emotions of all sorts to the mind. Besides the plants visible to the eye there will be in such a garden other comely growths, plain to that other sense, such as faith, romance, the lore of old unhurried times. These are infinitely well worth cultivating among the rest. These are an added joy in happy times and gently remedial when life seems warped and tired.

In the mid-1930s Miss Wilder certainly knew her way around the garden. Imagine what she would say in today's world of high-speed drama.

Many flowers need something other than simply blatant color or waving petals to generate an outside interest in their eventual pollination, and that superfluity is oftentimes fragrance. The fragrance is typically sweet, although a flower will occasionally produce a sweet-sour smell reminiscent of stale beer, or in the case of blossoms pollinated by many species of bats, of overripe fruit, or at worst, a distinctly musty odor much like that of a wild animal's den.

Any dog or cat owner knows the importance of smell to an animal's everyday activities. Dogs and cats find their way across vast distances using a combination of sight and sense signals, surprising everybody except those who have lived closely to these creatures.

Many psychologists believe that mankind's ability to recognize and remember an odor once matched that of animals, for mankind's sense of smell was far more pronounced thousands of years ago than it is today. We have lost the ability to recognize and mentally catalog literally thousands of odors. However, our weakened olfactory senses can quickly detect minute differences in a formula for perfume or the subtle changes in an aging bottle of wine. And we cannot overlook the continued popularity of the human scent — the body's production of pheromones, natural scents that are linked to sexual attraction. A burgeoning industry bottles these chemicals. Remember the popularity of musk?

In 1997 the AgBiotech Center of Rutgers University reported that tobacco plants give off clouds of oil of wintergreen, a volatile liquid that functions as an airborne signal warning neighboring plants of an infection of tobacco mosaic virus. Healthy plants that received the signals immediately built up supplies of salicylic acid, a chemical essential to plant immune activities.

Scientists have long noted that odors are particularly prominent in primitive plants and particularly strong in blossoms that are pollinated by beetles. Tropical nights, they write, are filled, almost beyond belief, with the fragrance of beetle-pollinated blossoms, including the powerful scent of the great Victoria water lily *(Victoria amazonica),* the sweet smell of the magnolia, and the rich odor of the nutmeg tree *(Myristica fragrans).* The rhythm of odor production indicates that even those pollinators with keen eyesight depend on the flower's fragrance as an olfactory road map, especially if the flower is small or drab in appearance. In essence, odors can work as the catalyst that in turn triggers the release of instinctive reactions in animals, particularly in insects.

FLORAL FRAGRANCE OF YESTERDAY

Dr. Robert Brown, a Scottish botanist of the 19th century, devised three classifications for floral odor: superodorants, subodorants, and nidorants. Superodorants include the perfumes that are agreeable to man, bird, and insect, the sweetest being the odors of the pinks, the orange, roses, the vanilla orchid, daffodils and narcissus, many of the lilies, violets, tuberoses, wallflowers, and the stocks.

Subodorants are flower smells that are less cheery but nevertheless agreeable. For this category, Brown picked flowers like the jessamine, acacias, and the flowers of the almond.

Brown's classification of nidorant includes the fragrance of the rues, garlics, a number of wildflowers called foxy (a salute to the strong odor associated with that animal's personal aura and often to its den), stapelias or carrion flowers *(Stapelia* spp.) and, in particular, the voodoo lily *(Amorphophallus* spp.), which smells so strongly of carrion that its presence soon makes any enclosed space an unbearable place to be. These plants bore flowers whose odors, when first smelled in English greenhouses, supposedly caused strong men to weep and stout British women to faint dead away.

Happily, the flowers described in this book are either superodorant or subodorant, or a combination of both. The nidorant have been left by the wayside.

FLORAL FRAGRANCES FOR TODAY

Fashions change, and the popularity of fragrances is no exception; one generation's most popular scent is an anathema to the next. But a few classifications seem to be constant.

1. Heavy is a fragrance classification that describes those sweet-smelling flowers (and perfumes) that can be overpowering at close range. In the flower category, mock orange (*Philadelphus* spp.), tuberoses, osmanthus, some lilies, and many honeysuckles come to mind. In his 1597 herbal, the English botanist John Gerard called the mock orange "too sweet, troubling and molesting the head in a strange manner." For those with a chemical frame of mind, these scents contain benzyl acetate, indole, and methyl anthranilate. Indole, found in the excrement of animals (including humans), points to the fact that life has always been a strange mix.

When it comes to perfumes, many of the cheaper brands are best described as heavy, and discretion is often the better part of valor regarding the high-priced varieties.

2. Aromatic represents those flowers possessing a spicy fragrance like the garden pink. The chemicals, among others, that conspire to create these odors include cinnamic alcohol, eugenol, and vanilla. (I can remember the marvels of taking the cap from a bottle of real vanilla and inhaling that marvelous sweet fragrance.) Many aromatic flowers, particularly nocturnal flowers, contain some of the chemicals found in the flower group classified as heavy — night-scented stock, nicotiana, many tropical orchids, heliotropes, and *Gladiolus tristis,* for instance. Surprisingly, while many of the orchids do have powerful scents, none of the plants in the aromatic group contain indole, so even if the flowers that produce these fragrances appear to be strange or even bizarre, their odor is never overpowering.

3. Lemon contains citral, a chemical found in oil of lemon, oil of orange, and bay leaves. Although it isn't common in the typical garden flower, lemon scent is very noticeable in magnolias, water lilies, many fragrant daylilies, and four-o'clocks.

4. Foxy is the term applied to the last category of flowers. This polite term refers to plants or blossoms that have a certain ferine odor, slightly musky but certainly not equal to the odor of a caveful of stegosauruses and not potent

The pink members of the rugosas (Rosa rugosa) grow with single or double flowers and range in blossom color from deep pinks to bright pinks to those with petals of a soft, clear pink. Most are delightfully fragrant.

enough to lead to the defenestration of the offending plant. When one tries to imagine the privileged haunts of the royal classes (forgetting about sties, privies, and local taverns) of most of the centuries leading up to today's age of soap and deodorant, you have some idea of just how harmless most of the plants that suffer with names like stinking, smelly, or foxy really are. Other than the leaves of a boxwood after a rain and a few tropical trees that are pollinated by bats, I can't think of any garden flower that fits this description.

Certain fragrances often remind us of that marvelous smell of clean clothes hanging on a washline to dry in the sun (not that fake ersatz odor conjured up by chemists and sold to today's housewives — and househusbands — as a necessary substitute for the disappearing backyard). And there are flowers that have the same type of refreshing smell: consider the daffodil or the narcissus or the shy violet in the early spring.

Then there are the so-called fragrances of horror, a term usually applied to the blossoms of the devil's-tongue (*Amorphophallus rivieri*) or the many leathery flowers of the Stapeliad clan. The pollinator is not a bee, wasp, or butterfly but one of the larger members of the ubiquitous fly family, and the smell is one of rotting meat or fermenting vegetables. The odor released by the devil's-tongue was once described as so disturbing and awful that brave women blocks away from Kew Gardens in London (where it first burst forth in the mid-1800s) fainted dead away.

Remember these lines by Joseph Joubert (1754–1824): "Scents are the souls of flowers: they can be perceived even in the land of shadows," and those by Arthur Symons (1865–1945): "Without charm there can be no fine literature, as there can be no perfect flower without fragrance."

Gladiolus tristis *grows wild in South Africa, where it is found at the borders of swamps and wetlands. The flowers are sweetly fragrant, especially in the evening.*

CHAPTER 2

GARDEN CARE AND MAINTENANCE

The plants described in this book range from those that are happy in water to those that prefer the driest of soils to those few that can survive in pure clay. To insure the best growth and the happiest flowers, make sure you know what kind of soil your garden will provide.

TYPES OF SOIL

As you plan a fragrance garden, check your soil for its character: is it solid clay, rich loam, or a combination of both? Is it well drained or does the water stand in puddles even after a light rain?

Clay soils are sticky. If you roll a lump of wet backyard soil between your fingers and it forms a compact cylinder that refuses to break up, it's clay. Clay isn't all bad, as it contains valuable minerals that plants need for good growth. When dry, however, clay can be rock hard, and instead of percolating into that soil, rain or hose water simply rolls to the lowest level.

The opposite effect occurs with sandy soils: water is absorbed so quickly that the soil is often dry within hours of a heavy rain.

Oleanders (Nerium oleander) *are shrubs that originated in the gardens of India. They perfume the summer air with the fragrance of almonds. Remember, all parts of this plant are poisonous.*

The best garden material is a good mix of soil and organic matter, much like that found in the woods, where leaves fall and rot over thousands of years. Plus, of course, good drainage. Of all the factors essential to good gardening, the most important is drainage.

There are many ways to improve your impoverished soil. You can add compost from your own compost pile; seasoned manure (fresh manure is usually too strong to plant in directly, so mix it in the soil thoroughly in late fall, winter, or very early spring, and wait a few months before direct planting); leaf-litter; or bags of composted manure, which can be found at garden centers.

RAISED BEDS

If your soil is really bad and not worth the effort to improve, how about making a raised bed? Instead of digging down, mark out your area and build it up about 2 to 3 feet above the ground level using railroad ties from the lumber yard. If you are not sure whether the ties have been treated with creosote (newer ties generally are free of the chemical), be sure to ask as it's dangerous to people and pets. You can even build a wall of concrete blocks, fieldstone, or even bricks. Then fill the new area with your own or purchased top soil.

If you live on the side of a hill, you can do this to build terraces and prevent the rain from washing down the slopes.

Our first country garden — in the Catskill Mountains of upstate New York — was located on a hill composed of granite with an overlay of red shale and a sprinkling of larger rocks. By building retaining walls of concrete blocks and topping them with a layer of fieldstones from nearby old stone walls (for good looks), we created good soil and perfect drainage, and we didn't have to stoop over for cultivation jobs or to pick flowers.

A NURSERY BED

If your garden is expanding and you wish to try new plants, especially those grown from seed, plan for a small nursery bed in your garden. It need not be large, but it should be in a protected spot, have good soil, access to water, and be out of the way so that you aren't under pressure to consider aesthetics. Here you can raise seedling plants to maturity before planting them in the garden proper.

Raised Beds for Wet Spots

When framing a raised flower or herb bed, large rocks provide an attractive contour. By raising the soil level, you give your flowers and plants more well-drained rooting room.

Drawings by Elayne Sears

WATERING THE GARDEN

The traditional rule of thumb is that gardens need 1 inch of water per week. Not many of us keep rain gauges in our gardens (although we should), and moisture needs change depending on weather conditions, soil type, plant type, and the surrounding environment. For example, there is more evaporation with high winds. Generally, if your garden gets a good soaking rain once a week, you'll be able to forget about watering. But gardens in fast-draining sandy soils may need additional water, as may gardens in hot climates. Plants summering outdoors in pots will also need to be watered daily, or perhaps twice a day, depending on the size of the pot. Shallow-rooted plants must have more water than deep-rooted varieties, and new plants require constant moisture to help establish fledgling roots. The best way to tell when the garden needs water is to stick your finger in the soil. If it feels dry a couple of inches below the surface, it's time to water.

Overhead sprinklers are the least efficient, especially in areas of high sun, high heat, and porous soil. Soaker hoses have tiny holes that release water slowly and are better than sprinklers. Drip irrigation systems are best because they deliver water directly to the root zone. Kits are available that include the necessary hose attachments. Just attach the system to a water source, install a timer if you like, and you're ready to go.

MULCH: KEEPING THE GARDEN MOIST

Each year it's more difficult to welcome the dog days of summer because with every new July or August, the sun beats down with increased strength, baking the soil and evaporating water. A garden mulch will help to conserve water and also cut down on the growth of weeds. And a neatly applied layer of mulch often looks better between the plants than parched dirt.

A number of mulches are available around the country, including buckwheat hulls, chopped-up corn cobs, marble chips, pea gravel, pecan hulls, pine bark chips, pine needles, and for those in love with the smell of chocolate, cocoa husks. You can also use garden compost, hay, and leaf mold (soft leaves like maple will mat, unlike the tough leaves of oaks). Never use peat moss; when completely dry it becomes a hardened mass that sheds water like a hot griddle scatters droplets.

In addition some people use black plastic but if you do, be sure and cover it with a less offensive material.

PROPPING THE PLANTS

Some plants grow well with stout and sturdy stems; others become top-heavy with fragrant blooms and have a habit of bending over, particularly during those sudden thunderstorms of summer. So it becomes necessary to prop them up. Here are four methods.

Pea-staking, an English invention, involves placing branches pruned from trees upright in a perennial bed early in the season. The plants grow up through the sticks and cover them with foliage. The branches should be 6 inches shorter than the leaves of the plant. We use birch, wild cherry, and maple taken from our neighboring woodlands. The name originated in the vegetable garden, where this method was used to support pea vines.

Wire plant supports, which originated in Scotland, consist of heavy concentric wire rings wrapped around three metal legs. The plants grow up through the rings.

Bamboo or reed stakes can be used to support single-stemmed plants. I gather all the stems of my eulalia grasses *(Miscanthus sinensis)* in late fall and use them with twist-ties or plastic clips.

Cat's-cradle is achieved by setting out four short corner stakes and winding green garden twine across and between.

CONTAINER GARDENING

Many of the plants described in this book will grow well in containers. Container plants are successfully grown by city gardeners with small terraces and suburbanites with small backyards.

A container, by definition, could be a small clay pot, a sunken soapstone sink, or a large raised bed. They all hold dirt that you will mix to your specifications, and the soil can be adjusted far more easily than that in an entire backyard.

I have an especially beautiful gardenia that is much too tender for our mountain winters, so I planted it in a terra-cotta pot. It is an attractive addition to the top of the stone wall in our side garden; when it blooms in mid-winter I bring it into the study, where it perfumes the entire room.

My first experience with container culture came from the wonderful book *Pots and Pot Gardens* by Mary Grant White. It is an English book, published in 1969, and although the pictures are black and white (horrors!), it fired my imagination.

According to Miss White's book, tomb paintings of ancient Egypt depict the use of earthenware pots for growing palms and grapes. Flowerpots from Ancient Greece look amazingly like present-day designs and hold not only a variety of decorative plants but also root cuttings for eventual planting around temple borders.

All the pots I use are earthenware — never plastic — and I immediately wash them after I empty them of their present inhabitants. The general soil mix consists of sharp sand, composted cow or sheep manure, and sterilized potting soil, one-third each. Make sure the drainage holes are present and open, using a bit of wire screening or even some paper towels folded two or three times to keep the soil from falling out.

Another special advantage to containers comes in the fall. On chilly nights you can either move them to a warmer and protected spot or cover the pots with some newspaper to keep frost from forming. And on those warm days of Indian summer, your fragrant garden will continue to delight you.

PESTS AND DISEASES

There is no perfection in nature, and, unless you work at it 24 hours a day, very little in the garden. Rather then using commercial pesticides (especially when their labels feature an 800 number to call if you're exposed to the package contents), I have always believed that a few chewed leaves or nibbled stems will not detract from the beauty of the garden. So rather than poison moles, I welcome their help in ridding the lawn of grubs, and when the garden is attacked by voles, I turn the job of policing over to our garden cat.

If the garden is suddenly under attack by more than just a few marauding insects, however, I will mount a counterattack using the following methods.

When dealing with aphids, I spray them directly with a bottled liquid cleaner, like Fantastik, let the soap sit for eight to ten minutes, then wash it off with the fine spray on the garden hose.

For Japanese beetles, I install scent traps. If they number only in the dozens, I pick them off by hand and put them directly into soapy water.

Our worst problem is the slug, simply one of nature's most disgusting creatures. These are snails, *sans* the shell, that glide about at night on a trail of slime, chewing holes in just about everything. I've tried slug traps baited with beer — I refuse to use poisoned bait because of possible danger to our garden cats (who effectively take care of the rabbit and vole problems) — but have never found them to work. Therefore, I resort to two easy methods. One: in the dead of night take a flashlight out to the garden, spotlight the slug, then sprinkle a few grains of salt on its tender body. The salt kills them without any damage to the garden. But use alcohol if you are tender-hearted, as the salt is a slow killer. Two: put a few pieces of damp cardboard or a wooden plank or two at the edge of the garden; during the heat of the day, slugs will gather there to enjoy the cool, damp dark. Then you can turn the cover over and kill the slugs.

Insects like flea beetles can be controlled by spraying with an insecticide derived from the dried flower heads of the pyrethrum daisy *(Chrysanthemum cinerariifolium),* a plant that resembles the common field daisy. With solvents the active ingredients are removed from the flowers, then dried and sold as a powdered concentrate that makes an effective spray. There is one problem with pyrethrum: it is readily broken down chemically by the action of light, often in a matter of hours, so apply this fix in late afternoon.

Rotenone is another plant-based insecticide, manufactured from the roots of the derris or tuba plant *(Derris elliptica)* and the lancepods *(Lonchocarpus* spp.), but it can cause severe irritation to humans if inhaled. Rotenone is sold as a dust and is an extremely potent control for many insect species. The killing action is slow, however, and like pyrethrum, it breaks down in the environment, although not as quickly.

Spider mites bite the dust when confronted with insecticidal soaps, bottled spray cleaners, or powerful bursts of water. Remember that the mites are always on the underside of the leaf, not on the top.

For those gardeners who have the inclination to carry the war directly to the enemy, there are firms who supply the eggs of ladybugs *(Hippodamia* spp.), praying mantis *(Mantis* spp.), and green lacewings *(Chrysopa* spp.) — troops that will wage the battle for you.

A WORD ABOUT CLIMATE ZONES

The United States Department of Agriculture (USDA) Zone Map (see page 115) is based on average *minimum* temperatures found in various parts of the United States and Canada (the map refers only to a plant's hardiness to cold weather, not to heat or other factors like drought or humidity). Even then, the zones are only guidelines. For a more accurate idea as to the highs and lows for your area, contact your county's extension service.

Microclimates are also important. These are areas sheltered from the worst of the winter winds, areas that receive protection from the grace of being behind a small hill, places that enjoy extra warmth provided by heat leaking from a nearby warm building foundation, or a spot that gets extra sunlight even on a sunny day in winter. One of the marvelous adventures of gardening is experimenting with plant placement and succeeding with a rare plant where other gardeners have failed because they did not provide that extra measure of protection.

Chapter 3
Annuals

Annual plants are the unsung heroes of the garden. For about the last ten years, they've played second fiddle to the perennials. But if you want to be a quick-sketch artist, annuals make the garden your canvas and the blossoms your paint.

Annual plants will germinate, grow, flower, and seed all in one season. Many of them complete this speedy life cycle in 12 to 14 weeks. As such, annuals are the closest thing to instant gratification in the garden, outside of purchasing a complete spread from a Texas department store. And there are a number of these fast-track plants that produce marvelous fragrances. A number of tropical plants that are perennial in warmer climes are treated as annuals in northern gardens. Unless noted, all of these plants will do well in any reasonably good, well-drained garden soil, usually in full sun except in the Deep South, where they will welcome some noontime shade.

Some Fragrant Annuals

The following plants can be found in most seed catalogs or garden centers; a few are available only from the smaller seed houses that specialize in more unusual plants. The following night-fragrant annuals are also mentioned in chapter 9.

Heliotropium arborescens, *commonly called heliotrope or cherry pie, is one of the most fragrant flowers you can grow.*

Pot marigolds *(Calendula officinalis)* were once grown not for their pungent leaves and stems and fragrant flowers but as pharmaceuticals for home-healers. The flowers grow as wide as 4 inches and are available in a wide variety of colors, such as orange, apricot, cream, and bright yellow. Although the long narrow leaves are slightly clammy to the touch, the blossoms are a delight to both eye and nose. Mass them in the garden or grow them in pots, being sure to remove spent blossoms to endure continued bloom. Start calendulas indoors six weeks before your last frost, or sow seeds directly in the garden as soon as the ground can be worked. Space dwarf varieties 8 inches apart and taller types about a foot apart.

Sweet sultans *(Centaurea moschata)* originated in the Orient. Plants bear sweet-scented thistlelike flowers, about 2 inches across, on 2-foot stems. They resemble cornflowers with fringed petals and come in various colors, including white, yellow, carmine, plum, and pink. Sow the seeds directly outdoors. For continued bloom, make successive sowings during the summer. Seeds germinate in ten days and bloom eight weeks from germination.

I first saw mention of these flowers in the 1936 edition of Taylor's *The Practical Encyclopedia of Gardening,* but it wasn't until 1991 that Thompson & Morgan carried the seeds. Either sow them directly in the garden or start them in peat pots as the plants resent root disturbance. They need some shade in the Deep South.

Queen Anne's pocket melon *(Cucumis melo)* is a small annual vine that grows no taller than 6 feet and bears 3-inch yellow flowers, followed by oval fruits that are green at first and then turn to yellow stripes on a brown background when ripe. Forget the flowers and grow this vine for the sweet perfume of the ripened fruit. It is said that good Queen Anne would carry this little melon in her reticule as she walked the rather dank palace halls, inhaling its fragrance now and then to be relieved from the various castle odors. For August fruit, start the seeds directly outdoors as soon as frost has passed. For an early start, you can plant seeds in 3-inch peat pots about four weeks before the last frost, using three seeds per pot and discarding the weaker two seedlings. A string trellis is quite adequate to hold the vine.

The thorn apple family of plants contains two species of annuals; the first is called angel's trumpet *(Datura metel).* The tall, rambling plants bear many foot-long trumpet-shaped cream-colored to pure white flowers, often 8 inches long and intensely fragrant. The plant is sometimes called *D. meteloides* when the flowers have a lavender tinge. The second plant is *D. stramonium*, a pantropic weed with ill-smelling foliage, spiny seed pods, yet beautiful, sweet-smelling white flowers, almost like the regular angel's trumpet. Try to grow the first and be very careful of the second. All are poisonous!

Start seeds six weeks before the last frost, using 3-inch peat pots with two seeds per pot. Remove the smaller seedling. Daturas will flower in 14 weeks from seed and do well in pots on a terrace. If the soil is too rich, you will get large healthy leaves and fewer flowers. Provide some shade on hot afternoons.

Sweet William *(Dianthus barbatus)* is a common pink plant that is grown for the beauty of the bunched and fringed flowers and for the marvelous fragrance. This particular plant, actually a biennial, has been a favorite since my great-grandmother's day. Look for the cultivars 'Indian Carpet', 'Summer Beauty', and 'Roundabout'. These new varieties will blossom the first year if the seeds are started early. Sow seeds indoors six to eight weeks before the last frost, then move seedlings to an outside cold frame when the weather has settled — they really like cool temperatures.

A perennial vine treated as an annual, Hyacinth bean *(Dolichos lablab)*, also known as the Bonavista bean, the Lubia bean, and the Indian bean, originated in the Old World and is considered an important food product in the tropics. These vines are rapid growers, making a run of 15 or more feet in one summer. The purple, pealike flowers are very fragrant, and after they mature they produce decorative pods about $2^{1}/_{2}$ inches long with the burnished look of an antique cello. Sow seeds outdoors as soon as danger of frost has passed, spacing plants 1 foot apart. They need a trellis or strings to climb.

Cherry pie, or heliotrope *(Heliotropium arborescens),* are sweet-smelling plants from Peru. They are perennials in their native haunts but are grown as annuals in most gardens. Blooming plants bear many small violet or purple flowers, each about a quarter of an inch long on 15-inch plants. The scent is usually described as being sweet and fruity, on the heavy side, and plants are grown in Europe for perfume ingredients. There is also a white-flowered cultivar called 'Alba'. In order for the plants to bloom in summer, their seeds should be started by the beginning of February. You can also buy plants from the nursery center (buy only one

The garden pinks (Dianthus *spp.) have been perennial favorites for centuries, not only for their bright flowers but also for their intense, spicy fragrance. The biennial sweet Williams* (Dianthus barbatus) *can be annual, biennial, or even perennial, depending on genetic background.*

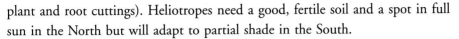

plant and root cuttings). Heliotropes need a good, fertile soil and a spot in full sun in the North but will adapt to partial shade in the South.

Rocket candytufts *(Iberis amara)* are aptly named as they often look good enough to eat. They are useful massed in the border, for edgings, and for cut flowers. The foot-high plants bear small, sweetly fragrant flowers in round clusters that resemble Victorian jewelry. As more flowers open, the clusters gradually become elongated, with seeds forming near the bottom of the stem. The colors vary from the traditional white with cultivars of pink, carmine, maroon, and rose now available. The variety 'Giant Hyacinth' has white blossoms on stems that reach 15 inches high. Sow seeds directly outdoors when the ground can be worked; for continued bloom, make successive sowings over the summer.

The moonflower *(Ipomoea alba)* is a perennial vine in the tropics but grown as an annual in most gardens. This is a vine that in good summer heat can reach 10 feet by late August but 40 feet in the typical jungle. The sweet-scented flowers are pure white with a faint touch of green along the floral fold. Each flower is 6 inches wide and 6 inches long. They open in early evening like a film in slow motion, sending a very sweet soapy fragrance into the night air. The vine flowers in eight weeks from seed, and the developing seed pods are also unique and interesting to watch in their development.

Sweet peas *(Lathyrus odoratus)* have been described both in poetic and garden literature for centuries. English gardens dote on their sweetly scented flowers but to many American gardens they are strangers because of their likes and dislikes. The plants climb by tendrils, usually no higher than 6 feet, and string trellises are a perfect foil. The 2-inch flowers come in a dazzling selection of colors, including white, pink, rose, red, maroon, yellow, and many bicolor combinations. All are intensely fragrant. They bloom from late spring to summer in cooler climates, but most everywhere else they stop blooming with the heat of early summer. Soak the seeds for 24 hours in tepid water before planting. Sow outdoors as soon as the soil is above 65°F or sow indoors, using individual peat pots as sweet peas resent any disturbance of the roots. Provide a half day of sun and use a fertile, well-drained but moist soil. They do well in pots.

Butter and eggs, also called meadow foam or poached egg flower *(Limnanthes douglasii),* is another American native annual from California. Inch-wide

saucer flowers with five yellow petals edged with white appear on the foot-high plants. The scent is lightly sweet, and the blossoms are extremely popular with bees. Plants prefer cool weather and moist, but not wet, soil. Sow seeds outdoors when the soil can be worked. Plants will often self-sow.

Sweet alyssum *(Lobularia maritima),* a perennial in its native home of southern Europe, is grown as an annual in most gardens. Older books call this plant *Alyssum maritumum.* The original color was white, but alyssum is now available in pink, lilac, purple, or rose. Look for 'Little Dorrit', only 4 inches high but covered with white flowers that smell lightly of sweet hay and honey. 'Rosie O'Day' bears sweetly scented rose-colored flowers. These plants are excellent as edgings along a garden pathway or tumbling over rocks in a rock garden. Sow seeds directly outside when the ground can be worked.

Pineapple weed *(Matricaria matricarioides)* is a weed of waste places that grows in the worst dirt imaginable and is gone by mid-summer. The finely dissected leaves are featherlike in appearance, and at the stem tips you'll see tightly packed conelike flowers without petals. Crush one of the plants and be amazed by the marvelous smell of pineapple.

Blazing stars *(Mentzelia lindleyi),* still listed in some catalogs as *Bartonia aurea,* are American natives from California that are perfect for growing along a rock wall or the edge of a pathway, as long as you provide full sun. The foot-high plants produce magnificent, almost 3-inch-wide flowers of bright shiny yellow that open in the evening (see chapter 9) and produce a marvelous spicy odor. The seedlings do not transplant well, so you should sow the seeds in place as soon as the ground can be worked. It is best to thin the plants to 6 inches apart.

Evening stock, or the perfume plant *(Matthiola longipetala),* is another weed lookalike with small, uninteresting flowers on nondescript plants. However, they produce a perfume of such beauty it can transform the night. The fragrance produced by these next-to-nothing flowers is a romantic combination of the heavy scent of jasmine and the light scent of aromatic flowers. These perfumes are produced by pink or purple four-petaled flowers with a white center, and looking for all the world like pieces of windswept, rain-washed tissue paper. To be sure that enough plants are available to scent your summer, set out new seed about every 10 days, at least to the middle of July.

Moonflowers (Ipomoea alba) *are sweetly fragrant, their pure white trumpets up to 6 inches across. Moonflowers bloom in early evening and fade the following morning, beginning their show of blossoms as the summer days get warmer.*

Sweet peas (Lathyrus odoratus) *have been featured in gardens for centuries. The newest cultivars offer finely scented blossoms, yet the older varieties boast the finest fragrances.*

Four-o'clocks *(Mirabilis jalapa)* are all-time favorites for the fragrant garden: they bloom in late afternoon with fresh, brightly colored flowers about an inch wide and 2 inches long on 2- to 3-foot bushes; they bloom from early summer until frost cuts them down; and finally, their flowers have a delightful lemony-sweet odor. Colors range from red to yellow, magenta, pink, crimson, white, and striped. Perennials in their native home of Peru, they are used as annuals, with seeds started about six weeks before the last frost and set out when all frost danger is past. The seedlings grow quickly and will overwinter outdoors except in

The desert star (Mentzelia lindleyi) *is a must in the fragrant border, not only for the color and sheen of the golden petals but for the sweet fragrance.*

cold climates. If you find a cultivar that is especially attractive, the tubers can be dug up and stored in winter like dahlias, then planted out the following spring.

Flowering tobacco plants have both day- and night-flowering species, including the large and stately tobacco plant *(Nicotiana tabacum)*, a species that will reach a height of 7 feet in the garden border. But best for the fragrant garden are the jasmine tobacco *(N. alata)*, *N. suaveolens*, and *N. sylvestris.*

Nicotiana alata is a perennial grown as an annual; it was originally imported from southern Brazil. Its flowers once opened about 6:00 P.M., but the flowers now stay open most of the day. The fragrance really explodes at night, though. Three cultivars are especially attractive: 'Grandiflora Alata' grows about 3 feet high, with large white flowers often 2 inches across; 'Lime Green', about 30 inches in height, with flowers the shade of lime sherbet; and 'Sensation Mixed' provides colors of maroon, red, white, and pink on 3-foot plants. If the plants get leggy at the end of summer, cut the mature stems back to a spot where they are enfolded by a leaf and give them a shot of liquid fertilizer; often new-flowering stems will appear.

Nicotiana suaveolens is an annual from Australia and grows a bit short of 3 feet tall. The 2-inch long, 1-inch-wide flowers are cream-colored, tinged with green on the outside. Rosemary Verey suggests growing it in pots so the fragrance can be enjoyed close to home.

Nicotiana sylvestris, a perennial grown as an annual, is the most fragrant of the group, sending out a sweet but decidedly heavy perfume. Originally from Argentina, this plant can reach a height just short of 5 feet, especially when grown in good-quality soil.

For all the tobaccos, start seeds indoors six weeks before the last expected frost. Once outdoors, plants like a location in full sun (they will tolerate some shade in the Deep South) and a soil liberally laced with compost or manure. For containers use a 12-inch-diameter pot, and in the heat of summer, always water at least once a day and apply fertilizer every month.

Most geraniums (*Pelargonium* spp.) are garden warhorses planted in pots, containers, and in public parks around the country. Most such plants bear blossoms with a bright and spicy scent, although they aren't usually considered fragrant plants. Scented geraniums, in the same genus but represented by a number of species, have small flowers, but their leaves can smell like pineapple, coconut,

Four-o'clocks (Mirabilis jalapa) *have long been the stars of the fragrant border, bearing beautiful sweet-smelling tubular flowers in a wide range of colors. They open in late afternoon.*

Nicotiana sylvestris *is a stout member of the nicotianas, originally from the Argentine, boasting lovely pendent white flowers that perfume the evening air.*

roses, almonds, lemons, apples, peppermints, ferns, and various citrus fruits. These leaves are often used to flavor cakes and jellies, to scent water for finger-bowls at fancy luncheons, and as ingredients in potpourri.

Among the scents available, look for *Pelargonium crispum* with its lemon-scented leaves; *P. quercifolium* smells of almonds, *P. tomentosum* of peppermint, *P. graveolens* of roses, and *P. odoratissimum* of apples.

This is Pelargonium *'Lemon Crispum'. Although the flowers of most geraniums lack fragrance, the foliage of the scented-leaved variety make up for this. Scents range from pineapple to cinnamon to peppermint; these geraniums are a marvel to the nose.*

Start seeds about 10 weeks before the last frost. After the first true leaves appear, move the seedlings to individual 2-inch peat pots, then to 4-inch pots as they grow larger.

Petunias *(Petunia × hybrida)* are often glossed over by most books dealing with fragrant flowers because many of the newer cultivars lack a strong perfume. The original plants, *Petunia axillaris* and *P. parviflora,* both imported from tropical America, were very fragrant, especially at nightfall. Today there are hundreds of cultivars, many coming true from seed and others propagated by stem cuttings. The colors vary from pure white, to pinks, reds, scarlets, blues, purples, yellow, and orange, some with picotee ruffles and some striped with color. Look for 'Blue Skies', one of the most fragrant cultivars.

If you grow petunias from seed, you will discover that only two or three plants in a dozen are delightfully fragrant. You might do better buying from a garden center, where you can smell every flat and choose those that still provide the fragrance.

Mignonette *(Reseda odorata)* is never really grown for the flowers, which look very raggy and weedy, but for the sweet perfume, an odor so delightful that plants are grown commercially for an essential oil used in perfumery. Plants usually grow about a foot and a half tall with heavy stems and spatulate, limp leaves. The small flowers are yellow-green to brownish yellow, in dense racemes, and nothing to write home about. But planted by the kitchen door, underneath a dining room window or picked for an indoor bouquet, they are wonderful. Seedlings resent transplanting, so sow them directly outdoors as soon as the ground can be worked. Do not cover, as the seeds need light for germination. Provide some shade where the afternoon sun is hot.

Reseda lutea is much more graceful in habit than others in the genus. Billed as an annual or a biennial, plants will flower the first year from seed if started early. They bloom most of the summer on 2-foot stems that bear small, light yellow flowers.

Pincushion flowers, or sweet scabiosa *(Scabiosa atropurpurea),* delight the gardener with sweet-smelling blossoms that are perfect 1-inch mounds of tiny blossoms, on slender stems of 2 feet or more, rising from a basal rosette of deeply divided leaves. Colors available are maroon, red, pink, rose, purple, deep purple (almost black), lavender, cream, or white. The unopened buds resemble fancy

The pincushion flower of sweet scabiosa (Scabiosa atropurpurea) *is a fragrant annual that will increase its bloom when deadheaded throughout the summer.*

colored raspberries or little Victorian brooches. 'Dwarf Double Mixed' are fully double flowers on stems to a foot and a half. Start seeds indoors six weeks before the last frost and plant out to a cold frame or a protected spot in early May, as the seedlings prefer cooler weather.

Poor man's orchids *(Schizopetalon walkeri),* little-known annuals of great charm, originally came from Chile. Deeply cut four-petaled flowers, three-quarters of an inch wide, have an unusually sweet fragrance and grow very well in

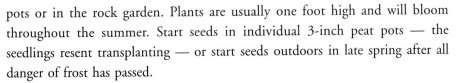

pots or in the rock garden. Plants are usually one foot high and will bloom throughout the summer. Start seeds in individual 3-inch peat pots — the seedlings resent transplanting — or start seeds outdoors in late spring after all danger of frost has passed.

Wind poppies *(Stylomecon heterophylla)* are a species of native plants from California and the Baja Peninsula. Flowers have four bright brick-orange petals with a large maroon blotch at the base of each petal and many yellow stamens in the center. The scent is reminiscent of lily-of-the-valley. Stems are up to 2 feet high. They are beautiful in the rock garden or planted in a seaside garden. Sow seeds directly outdoors in spring as soon as the ground can be worked.

Scented marigolds or the anise-flavored marigold *(Tagetes lucinda),* unlike the common marigolds that flood garden centers every spring, are really perennials originally discovered in Mexico. Plants can reach a height of 2 feet, with toothed, lance-shaped leaves and single orange-gold flowers that bloom in high summer. The whole plant is sweetly scented and leaves are used to flavor soups or dried for making herb teas. In colder climates, plants can be dug up before the hard frost and brought indoors for the winter. Indoors, sow seeds eight weeks before the last frost and plant out in a sheltered but sunny spot after frost danger is past.

Signet marigold *(Tagetes tenuifolia)* is another surprising member of the usually smelly marigolds, being small plants — about 1 foot high — with single, 1-inch wide flowers with yellow centers and surrounded by five yellow petals. 'Pumila' is the name applied to many dwarf and even more compact varieties of this plant. The foliage produces the fragrance of lemon verbena; it is considered by many gardeners to be one of the most delightfully aromatic of all annuals.

Nasturtiums (*Tropaeolum* spp.) are typically annual plants from the cool highlands of Central and South America. The common name is from the Latin for nose, *nasus,* and torture or twist, *tortum,* referring to the wry face that many

Garden nasturtiums, once called nose twisters, are annuals. They are delightfully fragrant to most and, if pesticide-free, can be added to salads. This is Tropaeolum majus *'Princess of India'.*

A FRAGRANT BORDER

The following flowers impart a mixture of sweet fragrance to the summer air. Although the heat of an average noontime will blunt the perfume of the blossoms, it will once again drift into the air as the afternoon passes and the sun sets.

The flowers chosen are flowering tobacco, both pink and white *(Nicotiana sylvestris* and *N. alata); various colors of sweet alyssum (Lobularia maritima);* nasturtiums *(Tropaeolum* spp.); mignonette *(Reseda odorata);* blue, rose, or white sweet scabiosa *(Scabiosa atropurpurea);* blue or white floss flower *(Ageratum* spp.); petunias *(Petunia × hybrida);* and for nighttime fragrance, the pink or blue flowers of the evening stock *(Matthiola longipetala)* and blazing star *(Mentzelia lindleyi).*

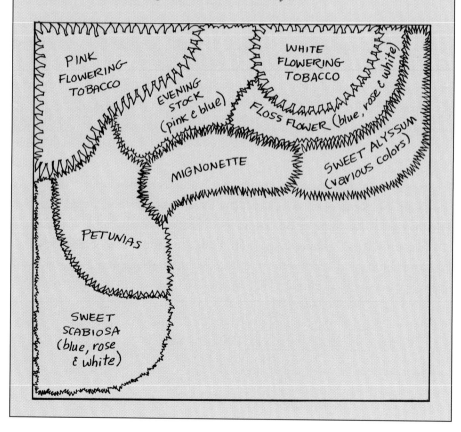

people make when biting into the leaves, which contain mustard oil. The leaves make great salad greens and young seed pods are often pickled like capers.

The dwarf nasturtium *(T. minus)* forms a small plant about 1 foot high, but the most popular garden subject is *T. majus,* a flower in cultivation for more than 300 years. Five-petaled and very fragrant funnel-shaped flowers, 2 inches wide and bearing a prominent spur, come in colors of deep red, mahogany, scarlet, orange, yellow, and white. The vines will grow 6 to 8 feet and are at home on a trellis, strings, or chicken-wire forms. They are also excellent in pots or containers where they can trail over the edge of a wall or just wander along the ground. Nasturtium leaves are fairly hardy, but seedlings are quickly killed by frost and do not transplant well; therefore, start seeds indoors in individual peat pots about two weeks before your last frost. Seeds need darkness to germinate. And, too, be wary of aphids. Nasturtiums are subject to almost overnight infestations of black aphids and before you know it, your entire collection will be savaged. Use a pyrethrum spray (see page 16) or spray the plants with a liquid cleaner, then wash off with the fine spray of the garden hose.

Two garden verbenas (*Verbena* spp.) are treated as annuals. The first is 'Homestead Purple', a cultivar discovered along a Georgia roadside, its mounds of glossy green foliage producing rich purple mounds of flowers, blooming throughout the summer, and gifted with a light sweet fragrance. The second, 'Texas Appleblossom', bears 2-inch heads of sweetly fragrant pink flowers, each with a tiny white eye. They are both excellent in pots or larger planters and do quite nicely as ground covers in full sun.

The night phlox *(Zaluzianskya capens),* an annual from South Africa, is named in honor of Adam Zaluziansky von Zaluzian (1558–1613). These beautifully fragrant, night-blooming flowers belong in every garden border or along the top edge of a wall. There the gardener can not only smell the fragrance but easily see the clusters of small, pretty phloxlike flowers. Each blossom is about a half-inch wide. The five white petals are notched at the top; when closed, both the petals and the outside of the floral tube are a satiny maroon with a hint of white showing where the petals overlap.

Chapter 4
Perennials

When considering fragrant flowers, the first reaction is to buy as many as possible. Think of going into a department store and upon reaching the perfume counter, opening every bottle and mixing the contents into one gigantic stew. The result would be unpleasant indeed. When mixing and matching fragrant flowers, the old dictum that "less is more" was never more practical.

The following plants are perennials; each has a fragrance of its own. Read the descriptions, mark those that seem to be appealing blends for the eye and the nose, then visit some of your garden friends. If you're lucky enough to live close to an arboretum that has display gardens, look at the plants in their natural surroundings. Unless noted they are all hardy in USDA Zone 5 and south.

Valerian, Jupiter's beard, or garden heliotrope *(Centranthus ruber)* is one of the dozen or so great plants for the floral border. It's a Mediterranean native, a summer bloomer, with tiny, very fragrant flowers in shades of salmon-rose, held high above gray-green foliage on 3-foot stems. Deadheading will encourage a second round of bloom. Provide well-drained, moist soil in full sun to partial shade. A white cultivar, 'Snowcloud', has an especially sweet perfume.

Red valerian (Centranthus ruber) *is a perennial with small red flowers that scent the air with a honeylike fragrance.*

The chocolate cosmos *(Cosmos antrosanguines)* is a fairly new perennial and this species is the hardiest member of the clan. The cosmos-type flowers bear petals of a rich reddish brown and stand aloft on 2-foot stems, making them excellent as cut flowers. But their best feature is the marvelous fragrance of chocolate. They are not hardy in areas north of USDA Zone 7, but I suspect you could store the roots just like dahlias in colder climates.

Garden, cottage, or border pinks *(Dianthus* spp.) are a hardy tribe of mat-forming ground huggers, with gray spiky leaves and marvelous five-petaled flowers redolent with the smell of sweet cloves. The cottage pinks *(D. × allwoodii)* bear 2-inch single, semidouble, or fully double flowers, with fringed petals, often with zigzag patterns, that bloom all summer long, if properly deadheaded. Cottage pinks *(D. plumarius)* grow in tufts of gray, pointed leaves, up to 4 inches long, and produce clusters of two to five single, semidouble, or double flowers up to an inch and a half wide, with spicy fragrances like a rich talcum powder. They, too, will bloom for long periods if you shear back the spent bloom almost to nearly ground level. 'Spring Beauty' is an especially attractive cultivar. These plants are great for beds, borders, rock gardens, and in pots, where they can be moved so that their fragrance will follow you from place to place. All the pinks need a sunny spot in fast-draining, neutral to alkaline soil; if planted in acid clay they won't last long.

The gas plant *(Dictamnus albus)* can be a problem in the garden because it really resents being moved. But once settled in, it will live for decades. The plants, which bloom in late spring to early summer, are about 3 feet tall and produce tall stems topped with unusual-looking, fringed rosy purple flowers with five petals. The crushed leaves have a citrus odor, often mixed with the scent of anise or sweet clover. The common name refers to the age-old belief that a gas plant leaf will produce a tiny gas jet when broken, and will ignite and burn on hot, humid nights. I tried it but then was told that the seed pods rather than the leaves or the flowers produce the gas.

Meadowsweet *(Filipendula* spp.) are large plants, some growing to 8 feet high. They bear spectacular heads of tiny fragrant flowers, with many stamens, above strongly cut foliage. When well grown, the Manchurian meadowsweet *(F. camtschatica)* reaches a height of 10 feet and salutes the nose with massive panicles of tiny fragrant white flowers. The European queen-of-the-meadow

The marvelous Allwood hybrid pinks were originally developed by the Allwood Nursery of Sussex, England.

The blossoms of the gas plant (Dictamnus albus) have been described as a blend of sweet clover and anise. The foliage has a distinct citrus scent. Squeezed seed pods emit a flammable gas that can be lighted on warm summer nights.

Many of the sunflowers have a pleasant, fresh fragrance. However, a few, such as the Helianthus grosseserratus, *have the distinct rich aroma of chocolate or cocoa.*

(*F. ulmaria*) is much shorter, barely topping 6 feet, and produces 10-inch plumes of fragrant creamy white flowers. In colder gardens it's necessary to provide a winter mulch, especially in areas with frigid temperatures but little snow cover.

The saw-toothed sunflower *(Helianthus grosseserratus)* is a native wildflower, a relative of the common garden sunflower, but one with a distinct difference: it smells of chocolate. In good soil, this plant can reach a height of 13 feet and is smothered with 2½-inch diameter blossoms from late September through early October.

The lemon lily *(Hemerocallis lilioasphodelus)* is one of the oldest plants in American gardens, brought over from Europe in the 1600s. Blooming in late spring, it's a most desirable plant, not only for the mound of foliage but the dozens of bright yellow daylilies it will produce and the sweet fragrance each flower provides. In some colonial gardens, its lush growth banished it to a spot by the kitchen door. The daylily cultivar 'Hyperion' is another hybrid famous for its rich honeysuckle scent, present from late afternoon well into evening. The true night-blooming daylily *(Hemerocallis citrina)* is listed in chapter 9 on evening-fragrant plants.

Sweet rockets *(Hesperis matronalis)* are short-lived perennials that have been garden delights for centuries. Dozens of half-inch flowers, arranged in showy terminal racemes, bloom with white, purple, or lilac petals. They are wonderfully fragrant, especially in the evening. Deadhead for continued bloom and raise new plants from seed every few years as the older plants become woody, then fade away. Provide a well-drained but evenly moist soil, and in the South, partial shade, especially from noontime sun.

Autumn-blooming hosta *(Hosta plantaginea)* usually blossoms from late August into September and in colder parts of the country the blossoms are often killed by an early frost. Originally from Japan (where it was introduced from China), this is a particularly valuable garden wonder with 5-inch-long, white, waxy, and fragrant flowers on 8- to 10-inch stems. A new cultivar, 'Aphrodite', boasts larger blooms than on the species.

The dwarf bearded iris *(Iris pumila)* is sweet-scented upon opening. With age the aroma becomes richer and much like ripening fruit. The floral stems are from 4 to 5 inches high and topped with iris blossoms in shades of white, yellow, and purple with a number of newer cultivars that expand the color choices. The best

Sweet rocket, dame's rocket, or hesperis (Hesperis matronalis) — *the latter named in honor of the evening star — is said to have been a favorite of Marie Antoinette. It's lovely by day and particularly fragrant by night.*

The autumn-blooming hosta (Hosta plantaginia) *was once called the old white daylily. Originally from China, it has a sweet scent that is strongest on cloudy afternoons and at twilight.*

Many of the Dutch and German iris (Iris spp.) have marvelous scents, particularly on warm spring afternoons. This is the lovely cultivar 'Artshades'.

place for this beauty is the rock garden, for the plants demand excellent drainage and a warm, sheltered spot.

Iris graminea bears flowers of yellow-white with purple veining, flowering in early summer on 18-inch stems, and provides the fragrance of ripe plums.

The orris iris *(Iris pallida)* has lavender-blue flowers, 4 to 5 inches wide, that have the distinct fragrance of orange blossoms and elderberry flowers. This is one of the plants grown for the production of orris, the powdered dry rhizomes that are used to make many perfumes.

Finally, the bearded iris *(Iris × germanica),* or the flag, has blue-purple falls with white beards, an amazing number of cultivars in colors from white to yellow to orange to blue. The height is between 2 and 3 feet, and plants do need a well-drained soil in a sheltered spot. The rhizomes of these irises are also a major source of orris.

Bee balm or Oswego tea *(Monarda didyma)* grows in upright to somewhat sprawling clumps, with 2- to 4-foot stems holding aloft tubular flower in dense clusters. Colors range from white to pink to red, lavender, and purple. These plants prefer a sunny location in a fertile, well-drained soil and are especially attractive in wild gardens where they are bound to invite bees, butterflies, and hummingbirds.

Phlox *(Phlox* spp.), whether short or tall, bear tubular flowers on strong stems, many being notably fragrant. The best garden phlox are hybrids of *P. paniculata,* plants with a great range of colors, from pure white to many shades of pink and red. 'Starfire' has blossoms of bright, bright red; 'Orange Perfection' bears salmon-orange flowers on 2- to 3-foot stems. The best white was, until recently, 'Mt. Fuji', with weather-resistant mounds of delightfully fragrant flowers. However, a new cultivar, 'David', provides flowers from mid-July until late September. Even if marketed as disease-resistant, phlox do require extra maintenance, especially if the summer lacks rain. Water deeply at the roots during dry seasons but avoid wetting the foliage, as all of these plants are susceptible to various mildews.

Peonies *(Paeonia* spp.) are flowers of great antiquity, the Greeks believing these splendid plants to be of divine origin. And not only are they beautiful to behold; many are extremely fragrant. The common garden or Chinese peony *(P. lactiflora)* was introduced into England in the mid-1700s and is the species that gave rise to most of the garden peonies of today. Their typical pure white

Bee balm, or monarda (Monarda didyma), *is known both for its marvelous clusters of brightly colored flowers and for the wonderfully scented leaves, which are used for herb teas and to scent hair pomades.*

flowers with golden stamens in the center are beyond description when crowded into a splendid vase and set on a table, and their fragrance will make its way around a room. Look for 'Marie Crousse' with fragrant pink flowers, the white 'Dutchesse de Nemours', the pale pink 'Sarah Bernhardt', and the species *P. delavayi,* one of the grandest plants of the tree peony family.

The catchword for growing great peonies is preparation. Before planting make sure the earth is well mixed with compost and dug deep. They also like a

Summer phlox (Phlox paniculata) *is noted for its beautiful flowers and sweet fragrance. This is the florific cultivar 'Harmony'.*

Nothing that spring can offer will rival the sweet scents of violets (Viola odorata), whether gathered for nosegays or simply flowering in the midst of a border or wildflower garden.

The yucca, or soapweed (Yucca glauca), is a large landscape plant that, once established, will live for decades. It produces tall panicles of fragrant flowers that are particularly sweet-smelling in the evening.

soil that is slightly limy rather than an acid type. Then, once installed, let them alone. They will persist for decades.

False Solomon's seal *(Smilacina racemosa)* produces 2-foot stems with terminal sprays of densely packed creamy white flowers in late spring. You can predict the fragrance by spying the dozens of small insects that flock to the stamens; they become so intoxicated they won't even know you're there. These native wildflowers want a moisture-retentive, woodland soil in light shade, especially in the South.

Violets *(Viola* spp.) bear single or double 1- to 2-inch flowers of blue, lilac, violet, yellow, mauve purple, or white. They are widely adaptable plants, often considered weedy, preferring sun to partial shade and well-drained, evenly moist humus soil. The most fragrant, and one of the best for the garden, is the sweet violet *(V. odorata),* a species that has a long relationship with both the florist and the perfumery. When buying cultivars, remember that the larger the flower is, the weaker the fragrance will most likely be. The horned violet *(V. cornuta),* originally from Spain and the Pyrenees and intensely fragrant, gets its name from the floral spur. Look for 'Arkwright Ruby' for maroon flowers and a great fragrance. They are not hardy above USDA Zone 6.

Yuccas *(Yucca* ssp.) have been favorites in my garden ever since I found that the richly sweet, white bell-like flowers are pollinated by a tiny moth that frequents only these flowers and ignores the others. One species in particular, the Spanish dagger *(Y. glauca),* gives the best floral show with pyramidal spires of pendant bells, 2 to 4 inches across, in clusters of hundreds. These plants need a sunny spot in well-drained soil. Once established they are drought-tolerant, able to last weeks without water from the rain or from the gardener.

CHAPTER 5

ROSES

I once looked up the number of references made about roses in the Fourteenth (1984) Edition of *Bartlett's Familiar Quotations*. The number was 267 for the singular form of the word and 134 for the plural. Quotations varied from Gertrude Stein's salute "A rose is a rose is a rose" to the song "Roses Are Blooming in Picardy" to Groucho Marx's immortal line, "Show me a rose and I'll show you the time of day." There's a reason: most civilized societies simple adore roses, both for beauty and for scent. A person standing in front of a blooming rose will almost always lean forward and sniff. Unfortunately there are a number of rose cultivars on the market today that might be big and blowsy when it comes to their blooms but painfully lacking in the scent department.

Because there are so many roses out there and so many claims to rose perfection, it's best to divide roses into categories. In each of the following category descriptions I offer suggestions for the best in fragrance.

SPECIES ROSES

Species roses began their garden tours of duty as wild roses collected from various places around the world. They are best described as having a genus and species name instead of a single-quoted cultivar or varietal term. Because they do

Although climbing roses must be attached to a support, once established they cover a multitude of sins. When they are close to a window, their marvelous fragrances easily brighten the room within.

Rugosas originally came from Japan but have been so successful at naturalizing that they are often assumed to be native plants. 'Alba' bears white fragrant flowers, large and single. The Rosa rugosa *'Alba' reaches a height of 6 feet.*

come from all parts of the world, hardiness varies, and they usually bloom only once a year with fragrant single flowers of five petals. Unless noted, the following are hardy except in the most severe circumstances.

Rosa carolina, or the pasture rose, is often found at the edges of abandoned fields, surrounded by tall grasses and wildflowers like black-eyed Susans. Plants grow about 6 feet high and bloom in mid-season with 2-inch-wide blossoms of a medium pink followed by attractive bright red hips.

Rosa eglanteria is the sweetbriar rose of Shakespeare's time. The bushes are between 8 and 10 feet tall, bloom early in the season with 1 to 1½-inch-wide blossoms of a light to medium pink, and have a true rose fragrance. Clusters of red hips follow, and, as an additional treat, the foliage has the fragrance of apples.

Rosa foetida bicolor, the so-called Austrian copper rose, is an early-season bloomer with petals of an orange-red on the top and yellow on the reverse. Although termed foetida, the smell is not all that bad, and while heavy, is like that of boxwoods. Some like it; others do not. Some gardeners think it is reminiscent of boiled linseed oil.

Rosa palustris, or the swamp rose, delights in wet, swampy soil, blooms late in the season with medium pink flowers about 2½ inches wide, and has a richly sweet scent.

Rosa rugosa is a champion of species roses. If I had my choice of only 10 plants for a fragrant garden, this rose would be one of those picked for the job. Originally found in northeastern Asia, this species has naturalized in the northeastern parts of this country. It is an excellent choice for making living fences (which will not overtake your garden). It produces large red hips, leaves that turn to attractive colors in the fall, lending a sense of architectural strength to any landscape. Marvelous mauve-pink 5- to 12-petaled blossoms go in and out of bloom for the entire season, and they are intensely fragrant.

A white form, *R. rugosa alba,* is identical to the species except for pure white flowers, and another, *R. rugosa rubra,* is characterized by flowers of a deep mauve-pink.

CLIMBING ROSES

Climbing roses include bushes that are easily tied to trellises, and roses that ramble, naturally called rambler roses. The following are the most fragrant climbers.

Rosa wichuraiana, 'Albéric Barbier', is a strong climber. Its long period of bloom features 3-inch white flowers with up to 55 petals and a fragrance reminiscent of green apples.

'America', a fragrant climber that is one of the few ever to win the AARS award (1976); plants reach a height of 9 to 12 feet and produce full, 4-inch double blossoms of coral salmon.

'Dr. J. H. Nicolas' is an 8- to 10-foot plant. Blooming with 5-inch medium pink blossoms, often with 50 petals, it is very fragrant.

'Golden Showers' reaches a height of 10 feet and blooms abundantly throughout the growing season with 4-inch medium yellow blossoms with up to 35 petals. It is very fragrant.

'New Dawn' was the world's first patented plant (1930). It grows to a height of 12 to 15 feet and becomes covered with fragrant light pink 3-inch blossoms of up to 24 petals.

'Veilchenblau', originating in the early 20th century, is often found in old gardens. The height is up to 12 feet, and the plant bears violet flowers with a white center that grow a little over 3 inches wide in mid to late season. The flowers bear the scent of sweet green apples.

SHRUB ROSES

Shrub roses are divided into a number of classes. For purposes of the average gardener they are best described as either small, medium, or large shrubs.

'Agnes' grows about 5 feet tall and bears 3-inch light yellow double roses, with up to 30 petals, blooming in midseason and often blooming again. The flowers are very fragrant.

'Belle Poitevine' is a shrub up to 9 feet tall and often as wide, with up to 4-inch, medium pink flowers of 18 to 24 petals, and very fragrant with the decided scent of cloves.

'Constance Spry' is named in honor of the well-known English garden writer, who both collected and popularized old garden roses. This is a 5-foot shrub with a long midseason bloom of 5-inch-wide medium pink blossoms that are very fragrant and said to smell of myrrh (something we've all read about, but I doubt if many of us have ever smelled it).

'Marigold' is excellent for the small fragrance garden, as it reaches a height of only 5 feet. From early to midseason, the plants bear fragrant deep yellow roses, about 4 inches wide with 14 petals.

'Penelope' grows between 5 and 7 feet high and bears pale extremely fragrant coral-pink blossoms, about 3 inches across, with up to 24 petals.

'Roseraie de l'Haÿ' is a large hybrid rugosa rose named for a famous French rose garden. Plants reach a height of 9 feet and bloom very early in the season. The dark reddish semidouble roses, over 4 inches across and with up to 24 petals, are very fragrant.

Old Garden Roses

Here is another catchall phrase that includes a number of rose types, including alba roses (descendants of a natural cross between *Rosa alba,* the white rose, and *R. canina,* the dog or briar rose); bourbon roses (discovered on the Isle of Bourbon, now called Reunion Island); centifolia roses (from Holland); China and tea roses; damask roses (hybrids of *Rosa damascena*); gallica roses (actually grown by the Romans); and moss roses (named for the green or brown mosslike growth on both buds and stems). From the hundreds of old garden roses, I've picked the following as favorites for both color and fragrance. When you give one of these roses a spot in your fragrance garden, you are truly dealing with a piece of history.

'American Beauty' has deep pink double blooms with 50 petals, 5 to 6 inches wide, that flower in midseason and again later in the fall. The plants are between 5 and 6 feet high.

'Baronne Prévost', a marvelous rose, goes back to 1842. Plants are about 5 feet high, bearing 4-inch double roses that can sport up to 100 petals. Bloom is midseason with good repeat bloom in the fall.

'Blush Noisette', introduced in 1817, has 2-inch-wide blush white flowers with 24 petals. It blooms in midseason and usually repeats in the fall.

'Celestial', a very sweet-smelling old rose of uncertain date, has light blush pink blossoms. It blooms very early in the season with semidouble flowers bearing up to 25 petals. Plants are up to 5 feet high.

'Common Moss', the old pink moss rose, is of an unknown origin. The sweetly fragrant flowers are 3 inches wide, with close to 200 light to medium pink petals. There is a heavy growth of green moss on the outer layer of the buds and stems. The moss is sticky and pine-scented.

'Gruss an Teplitz' roses are over 3 inches wide, with up to 40 rich medium

red petals. The midseason bloom is followed by a good repeat bloom. The bushy plants are between 5 and 6 feet tall, and the fragrance is strong and spicy.

'Henry Nevard' bears dark red flowers with up to 30 petals. The midseason bloom is followed by a good repeat bloom in the fall. These roses are very fragrant. The plants are between 4 and 5 feet tall.

'Königin von Dänemark' is an alba rose introduced in 1826. The flowers are about 3½ inches wide, of a light pink, with a deeper pink center. They are very double and display perhaps up to 200 petals. Bloom is early, without a repeat, but the intense sweet fragrance brightens up the dullest of springs. Treelike plants reach a height of 6 feet.

'Maiden's Blush' was known before the year 1600. Along the historical way, this rose has been called La Virginale, Incarnata, and Cuisse de Nymphe. I should think that most people would want it in their garden. The 3-inch roses are a light blush pink, very double in form, with more than 200 petals. They bloom in profusion at midseason and are extremely fragrant.

'Reine des Violettes', or the Queen of the Violets, was introduced in 1860. The color is usually lavender, but depending on the garden and the light, it may shift to shades of mauve. The 3-inch-wide blossoms are doubles with up to 75 petals, blooming in midseason, and sometimes repeating in the fall. The flowers are very fragrant and some authorities report that the foliage has a pepperlike fragrance, but I've never detected it. Plants are between 5 and 6 feet high.

'Rosa Mundi' has been known since before 1581. It's a striped sport of *Rosa gallica officinalis,* the apothecary rose or the red rose of Lancaster, and named for Fair Rosamund, the mistress of King Henry II of England. There are no two ways about it: this is a beautiful rose, and in fact is the earliest and most beautiful of all the striped roses. No two blossoms are marked in the same way. Sweetly fragrant flowers open in midseason, are up to 3½ inches wide with 18 to 24 petals, eventually opening to surround a mass of golden stamens. Round red rose hips appear later in the summer.

HYBRID TEA ROSES

Many professionals now call these large-flowered roses, while everybody else calls them hybrid teas. They are the roses that people usually imagine when thinking

Wheher small or large, a rose garden of mixed colors and mixed fragrances not only charms the landscape but provides cut flowers for an elegant dining table — not to mention an occasional corsage.

of roses. They are the most popular of all, great for cutting, and many will happily grow in tubs and containers. Unfortunately, fragrance has often been traded in for size of bloom. However, a few still can be grown for their exceptional perfume. Look for the following roses that, unless noted, are also disease-resistant and winter-hardy.

'Fragrant Cloud' has double flowers of coral red, 5 inches wide, on upright plants that grow 4 to 5 feet tall. They are excellent for all-season bloom, and their fragrance is intense.

'Friendship' received the All-American Rose Selection Award (AARS) for 1979, and for good reason. These rose blossoms are almost 6 inches across, medium to deep pink, an all-season bloom, with fragrant flowers rising above 5- to 6-foot plants.

'Kaiserin Auguste Viktoria' is one of the oldest hybrid teas (it was introduced in 1891) still in cultivation. The 4-inch-wide flowers are creamy white and full of petals (usually more than 100), are fairly constant with repeat blooms, and are very fragrant.

'Medallion', a 1973 AARS winner, is a classic rose that likes cool weather; as a cut flower, it enjoys a very long vase life. The light apricot flowers are more than 5 inches across, with up to 35 petals. It blooms in midseason and often repeats. The fragrance is rich and fruity. In cold climates, it needs good winter protection, including heavy mulching.

'Oklahoma', on the other hand, is a hardy and classically formed rose, a double with as many as 55 petals of a deep maroon red. These roses have an abundant all-season bloom and are very fragrant.

While the 'Peace' rose is often called the rose of the century, a winner of many awards in the U.S. and abroad, it has only a slight fragrance. 'Pink Peace', however, is something else again. Here is a blossom up to 6 inches across, with more than 50 petals of medium to deep pink riding on top of 5-foot vigorous and bushy plants. It is a very fragrant rose.

'Tropicana' was another AARS Award–winner and the first pure rose of fluorescent orange. It is often described as the third-greatest-selling rose in this century. Blossoms are 5 inches across with 30 to 35 petals of bright orange; they have a rich and fruity scent.

PESTS AND DISEASES

Like any other living thing roses are prone to diseases and pests; just like a healthy gardener, though, a healthy rose can put up with a lot while a weak rose will often succumb to whatever attacks.

Among the diseases waiting in the wings are powdery mildew, that dusty fungal growth that runs rampant during hot, humid weather. Remove badly infected leaves, try to increase air circulation, and check with your garden center for a sulfur-based dusting powder.

Virus attacks turn healthy leaves into something deformed and stunted. Remove and destroy infected plants, make sure that your shears are sharp and clean, and buy healthy plants from reputable sources.

Rust is a fungus that causes powdery orange spots on the undersides of leaves. Remove and destroy infected leaves and check for a suitable dusting powder at the garden center.

Aphids are soft little green or brown insects that suck the life out of plants. Wash them off with a powerful spray of water from the hose. If this doesn't work, try one of the liquid cleaners like Fantastik or an insecticidal soap.

Japanese beetles love rose foliage. Use traps to collect, then destroy.

Spider mites are tiny red, brown, or golden relatives of spiders that form on the undersides of leaves, spin many tiny webs, suck the life out of the leaf, then breed like mad, eventually unleashing millions of pests in your garden. Spray the bottom of the leaves with a hard spray of water from the hose and keep it up daily for at least two weeks.

CHAPTER 6
BULBS, CORMS, AND TUBERS

Botanically speaking, a bulb is a modified stem that contains an entire plant from leaves to bud; you can see it by slicing an onion vertically. A number of root types are linked with bulbs, including corms and tubers. While differing in structure, they share a common trait — the ability to store reserve food against a horticultural rainy day. Luckily for the gardener, a number of these bulbous plants have fragrant flowers. The following are just a few of the choices available. I have left out a few of the common fragrant bulbs like hyacinths and paperwhite narcissus in order to mention the more unusual ones.

Lily-of-the-valley *(Convallaria majalis)* are actually not bulbs but pips, but like roses, by any other name they would smell as sweet. These charmers can be used in beds, borders, rock gardens, and as ground covers. They make lovely cut flowers, not to mention their importance as a perfumery plant. Brought over by colonists, they have been in America since the 1600s and used as ground covers in cemeteries. The sprays of tiny nodding bells appear in late spring or early summer and can be forced into early bloom in a window garden by potting pips in the fall and keeping them cold for eight to twelve weeks. There are double forms, which I think of as unnecessary, and a form with pink flowers that, while dif-

Lilium 'Black Beauty' is a stunning flower; the fragrance of its blossoms turns it into a garden treasure.

Lily-of-the-valley (Convallaria majalis) *will fill the May garden with its light and airy scent. It is often used in perfumes.*

ferent, is rather pleasant in the garden. It should be noted that in such a delightful plant the berries and the rootstocks are poisonous. Lily-of-the-valley are cold-hardy from Zone 4 south but do not like areas with very warm weather, like the Deep South.

Crinum, or spider lilies, have spectacular scented blossoms. This hybrid between Amaryllis belladonna *and* Crinum moorei *bears beautiful flowers.*

The crinums (*Crinum* spp.), members of the amaryllis family, present the gardener with big, bold bunches of drooping lilies. There are a number of species available, but I recommend a magnificent hybrid between *Amaryllis belladonna* and *Crinum moorei* that results in the name × *crinodonna,* 'Summer Maid'. Unless

you live in USDA Zone 8 or south of it (thickly mulch the bulbs in Zone 7), this is a pot plant for you. And what a plant! In late summer, fountains of shiny straplike leaves (attractive even without flowers) suddenly become a backdrop for tall, thick, 3-foot stems that carry clusters of soft pink, very fragrant blooms high in the garden air. Overwinter the pots in a cool dry spot and water every month or so.

Freesias (*Freesia* spp.) are members of the iris family and hail from South Africa. I was introduced to these intensely fragrant flowers one bleak day in March, when a local florist showed me pots of very tall leaves — all tied up with string — that surrounded sprays of nodding waxy yellow flowers. They are easy to grow in containers (or outdoors in Zone 9 and south) by planting six pre-cooled corms to a pot, watering well, then leaving them alone for ten days. As the leaves develop, stake them to prevent their flopping over. The Dutch now supply precooled bulbs for planting outdoors in the summertime, too.

The garden lilies (*Lilium* spp.) represent a large genus of bulbous plants that are relatively easy to grow, both in the garden or, if space is limited, in pots. The majority of blossoms produce a rich and marvelous scent. Madonna lilies *(Lilium candidum)* have flourished in gardens since the days of the Minoan culture, fifteen hundred years before the birth of Christ. Medieval gardens had whole corners dedicated to these symbols of purity. The immaculate white and fragrant flowers perch on top of stems that may grow up to 6 feet tall, with up to 15 flowers per stem. Unlike other lilies, these plants need only an inch or two of soil over the top of the bulb. They should be heavily mulched in areas with very cold winters but little snow cover.

Last summer on a rainy afternoon, I went out to check a large clump of the gold-banded lily *(Lilium auratum)* blooming at the edge of my fern garden. Not only were they fragrant, but the heady smell could be detected from 15 feet away.

Lilies have been the stars of the fragrant border for generations. The sweet perfume of the Madonna lily (Lilium candidum) *is revered the world over.*

For late-summer bloom, try the fine *Lilium formosanum* with its elegant, 6-inch-long white blossoms that bloom on 4- to 6-foot stems. 'Little Snow White' is a cultivar from Taiwan with a large flower on a 9-inch stem. If grown from seed sown in September, this lily will bloom the following summer.

The most important thing to remember about lilies is that, unlike other bulbs, they are never dormant and the scales that surround the bulb have no protective covering and are easily broken. Handle them with care when planting. A few species, like the Madonna lily, want shallow planting, but most of the other species and cultivars have flowering stems that produce roots as they grow up to the surface; set them 4 to 8 inches deep. If your soil is heavy, dig the hole a bit deeper and put some sand at the bottom, then place a teaspoon of bone meal in the bottom of each hole. After inserting the bulb, add about an inch more sand before covering it with soil.

The tuberose *(Polianthes tuberosa)* was once one of the most popular fragrant plants in the civilized world. Unfortunately, because it became popular as a funeral parlor flower, it fell out of public favor. Today, of course, we can forget the past and again plant a few bulbs in the summer border or in pots for the terrace, and the marvelous sweet scent will again delight the senses. There are two varieties: 'Mexican Everblooming', which reaches a height of 4 feet and bears 2-inch-long waxy white extremely fragrant flowers, and 'The Pearl', which is 16 inches high and bears 2-inch double flowers. The bulblike bases are really rhizomes, as these plants are in the same family as yuccas and agaves. Unless you live in an area where the ground doesn't freeze (Zone 9), store the roots in a warm dry place during the winter. Tuberoses can be forced for November bloom.

The summer hyacinth *(Galtonia candicans)* struggles in the truly cold parts of the country but in USDA Zone 6, and warmer, it does beautifully. You do not have to dig them up in Zone 6. Forty-inch stems bear 20 to 30 fragrant bell-shaped flowers of white with a touch of green at the base. The individual flowers look like spring hyacinths, but are, to my mind, far more attractive. If snow cover is scarce in your garden and you don't have time to mulch heavily, plant the bulbs in mesh bags and dig them up for storage in the winter. It's worth the effort.

Species tulips (*Tulipa* spp.) are little-known bulbs often outstepped, but not outclassed, by their bigger relatives, the cottage and Darwin tulips, those bright

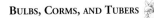

The summer hyacinth (Galtonia candicans) *is a taller but more demure version of the flowers blooming in the spring. The 2-inch white nodding blossoms are sweetly fragrant.*

The species tulips are smaller than their cousins that are often featured in spring displays, but they offer sweeter fragrances in return for daintier blossoms. This is the species Tulipa sylvestris.

and blowzy blossoms so loved by spring flower devotees. Species tulips are perfect for edges of the wild garden, for the rock garden, between paving stones, and in pots. They want full sun, well-drained soil, and summer heat.

The following are three of the most fragrant species. In Iran and Syria, *T. aucheriana* is found on rugged mountain slopes, producing one to three scented flowers from each tiny bulb. The star-shaped flowers open flat on 4-inch stems, and each pink petal has a yellow blotch at the base. From Asia Minor comes *T. batalinii,* available in a number of cultivars, including the most beautiful 'Red Jewel', 'Yellow Jewel', and 'Bronze Charm'. The latter variety adds a glowing bronze hue to the early-spring garden. Another fragrant beauty is *T. celsiana persica,* naturalized in Spain, France, and Morocco, with petals of a clear yellow and outer petals lightly tinged with bronze. Finally, *T. sylvestris* hails from West Africa and southern Europe and produces many yellow flowers, pendent in bud but standing upright in bloom. Because they are sweetly scented, they should be planted at the edge of a path or along the top of a garden wall.

It should be noted that unscrupulous bulb companies still gather these bulbs from the wild. So buy them only from catalogs that stipulate the bulbs are *propagated* at the nursery.

Chapter 7
Fragrant Shrubs and Vines

The following shrubs and small trees have been chosen to combine fragrant flowers, good form, and small stature. As such, they are well suited for the typical backyard. The vines are all reasonably well behaved, except for the Oriental wisterias; the dangers of growing these fragrant beauties is well documented below.

White forsythia *(Abeliophylum distichum)*, a 1924 shrub introduction, was first imported from central Korea. Searching for a popular name, some nurseryman decided on the white forsythia, a term that certainly describes the flowers but is botanically incorrect. However, this shrub is a prize addition to any garden no matter what you call it. The lovely white flowers are heavily fragrant, opening in early spring. If cut earlier in the season, they can be forced for indoor bloom. After flowering, the shrub becomes an excellent backdrop for other garden perennials. Flower buds appear in late summer, so prune in the spring after blossoming is over for the year. Provide ordinary garden soil. This beauty is hardy from Zones 5 to 8. It does not do well in areas where the summers are exceptionally warm.

The sweet pepper bush, or summer sweet (Clethra alnifolia), *bears terminal spikes of white blossoms that can scent the entire neighborhood when in bloom. This is the cultivar 'Paniculata'.*

*Butterfly bushes (*Buddleia *spp.) are available in a wide range of colors. The sweet-smelling blossoms are all loved by butterflies. B. davidii 'Black Night' has large bunches of purple flowers.*

Butterfly bush (*Buddleia* spp.). If you garden in Zone 5, butterfly bushes die back every winter, only to burst forth in the spring; in the South, they should be cut back to the stature of a short bush. By summer, they produce florific racemes of small, fragrant little flowers that are endowed with nectar that is especially attractive to butterflies. Happily, these bushes are not fussy as to soil. However, like most plants, they do appreciate good drainage, and while liking full sun, they will adapt to partial shade, especially in the South.

Carolina allspice *(Calycanthus floridus)* bears somewhat strange, reddish brown leathery-petaled flowers that open flat and are extremely fragrant. They are deciduous, losing leaves in the winter, but are quite beautiful in the formal or wild garden. Be sure to keep them close to any garden path so that you can enjoy their scent. Height varies between 4 and 10 feet, and they can be pruned in late winter or early spring to keep them within bounds. Soil should be well drained and evenly moist. The allspice prefers full sun in the North and woodland conditions in the South.

Fringe trees *(Chionanthus virginicus)* are one of my garden favorites. According to location, they could be termed large shrubs or small trees, eventually reaching 20 feet in height and width but easily kept within bounds with pruning. The fringelike white flowers bloom in spring; they are 4-petaled in 6-inch clusters. They send out a sweet fragrance, especially through shaded woodland gardens. Blue berries appear in the fall. In the garden next door, Doan Ogden wanted a Japanese look to his garden, so he weighted down a fringe tree with ropes and concrete blocks until it stayed in a bent position; it now frames the entrance to his moss garden. Fringe trees are hardy from USDA Zone 5 to 8.

The daphnes (*Daphne* spp.) are small, deciduous, evergreen shrubs that bloom with half-inch flowers packed into terminal heads. The flowers come in a variety of colors that range from white to pink to purple. Many species are intensely fragrant. These shrubs prefer sun to partial shade in the Deep South and they like humusy, well-drained soil that's on the slightly moist side. They are perfect as small specimen plants, in borders, in rock gardens, and in containers.

My favorite is the winter daphne *(Daphne odora),* a shrub that blooms in late winter and reaches a height of 3 to 4 feet with a 3-foot spread. The blooms are very fragrant, rosy purple without and white within. 'Variegata' has leaves edged with dashes of a creamy white tint. They are slow to establish themselves and resent areas with a hard winter.

Blooming when very young, the fringe tree (Chionanthus virginicus) *bears loose panicles of fragrant white flowers that glisten with a silvery sheen.*

Sweetspire *(Itea virginica)* are shrubs or small trees, between 8 and 16 feet in height, again according to location and pruning. The tiny fragrant white flowers in drooping foot-long clusters bloom in late spring or early summer. This is a marvelous plant for the back of the border so that the scent can drift over the garden's edge and be available to passersby. Soil should be well drained and evenly moist. They are hardy from USDA Zone 5 to 9.

Sweetspire, or the Virginal willow (Itea virginica), *bears drooping clusters of pure white fragrant flowers during early summer. This is the cultivar 'Henry's Garnet'.*

Oregon grapes (*Mahonia* spp.) are broad-leaved evergreen shrubs that look like hollies but are really members of the barberry family. They range in height from 3 to 10 feet and usually bloom in late winter to early summer with fragrant 3- to 6-inch drooping racemes of small buttery yellow, waxy-petaled blossoms. These are followed in the fall by purplish-black fruits, rather like small, pointed grapes, that last through the winter if your bird population doesn't find them. Bushes are hardy from USDA Zone 6 to 9. They prefer a well-drained, evenly moist, acidic garden soil. Cut them back after flowering, and even old bushes will send up new growth. The Japanese mahonia *(M. japonica)* is a recommended species, but *M. aquifolium* and *M. bealei* are both excellent additions to the garden.

Mock orange shrubs have sweetly scented flowers that, like old-fashioned peonies, often remind us of childhood. This is Philadelphus coronarius *'Natchez'.*

Mock oranges (*Philadelphus* spp.), old-fashioned deciduous shrubs from 4 to 12 feet in height, are known for their extremely fragrant white flowers. A good shrub may become so loaded with white cup-shaped flowers that its branches will bend under the weight. The common mock orange (*P. coronarius*) has very fragrant flowers and is represented by a number of cultivars, hardy from Zone 5 and south; some grow to 10 feet and others are quite short. A hybrid between *P. coronarius* and *P. microphyllus* produced the cultivar 'Avalanche', bearing white flowers that are exceptionally rich and sweet. Provide well-drained soil and a spot in full sun in the North and partial shade in the South. Thin out overcrowded shoots after flowers fade but be careful of young shoots as they bear flowers the following year.

Lilacs *(Syringa vulgaris)* arrived in American in the middle 1600s. The word is old, taken from the Arabic *laylak* and the Persian *nilak,* this last from *nil,* mean-

When lilacs bloom, they charm both the eye and the nose. Syringa × hybridus *'Exel'*
is a fine cultivar, characterized by early and fragrant flowers.

ing blue. By 1960, there were about 600 known cultivars produced in seven distinct colors: white (including cream), violet, lilac, blue, pink, purple, and red. There are also single and double flowers. "When lilacs last in the dooryard bloomed," Walt Whitman wrote in the mid-1800s. The flowers are lovely, the fragrance quite wonderful. Among the more attractive cultivars are 'Ellen Willmott', bearing double white flowers; 'Belle de Nancy', with flowers of double pink; and for those with limited space, *S. patula* 'Miss Kim', a Korean lilac of small stature (5 by 5 feet when mature).

Lilacs need a reasonably fertile, well-drained soil, preferably with a good organic content. Lilacs should be deadheaded to save energy and also for cosmetic reasons. If an old bush is cut way back, it may be three years before new flowering begins.

VINES

The vines listed below all have very fragrant flowers, and except for the Oriental wisterias, can be kept within bounds merely by selective pruning.

Except for the bush varieties *(Clematis heracleifolia),* clematises are vining or semi-woody climbers. A number are fragrant but three special species immediately spring to mind. All clematises like a slightly sweet soil, so when you plant, add a bit of limestone to the soil. In the North they appreciate full sun, but in the South some shade. It should be noted that all clematis like a cool root run: the vines might prefer the light, but the base of the plant where it enters the earth appreciates a shady, slightly moist spot.

The winter-blooming clematis *(Clematis armandii)* is very special because it blooms in midwinter and also because its evergreen foliage is beautiful without the flowers. Unfortunately, it is not hardy north of USDA Zone 7, and even there it can suffer if subjected to chill and below-zero winds.

The sweet autumn clematis *(Clematis maximowicziana,* formerly *C. paniculata)* blooms in early fall with hundreds of small, white, sweet-smelling blossoms. This vine is especially magnificent when allowed to climb its way to the top of evergreen trees, to which it does no harm. Zone 5.

Clematis heracleifolia davidiana is a bush-forming showy species that blooms with dense clusters of deep blue fragrant flowers on 4-foot stems.

Even though the sweet autumn clematis (Clematis maximowicziana) *is a vine with
a ponderous scientific name, the panicles of small white flowers are sweet enough to
scent late-summer afternoons.*

The Oriental wisterias bear marvelous drooping panicles of delightfully fragrant flowers. The vines, however, can threaten buildings. Here, Chinese wisteria (Wisteria sinensis) *is properly grown on a fence.*

Carolina jessamine *(Gelsemium sempervirens)* is an evergreen vine that needs warm winters to survive (it's only reliably hardy from Zone 7 and south). From late winter to early spring, a mature vine is covered with hundreds of tubular, fragrant, sunshine yellow blossoms that are especially noticeable when growing in the wild along the wooded edges of the interstates. This vine is easily grown against trellises, on fences, or naturalized. Gardeners in areas of Zone 6 and below can grow it in containers.

The honeysuckles *(Lonicera* spp.) are shrubs or vines, known for their honey-sweet flowers. Among the most fragrant vines are *L. japonica* and *L.* 'Halliana'. Unfortunately, they are also the most invasive, with the ability to reach over 30 feet, depending on the climate. If you have the space (and the strength) for this vine, allow it to scamper up a dead tree trunk or twine around a stout trellis. And nothing is better to carpet a difficult bank or a bare slope that has resisted everything you've planted. But be warned — they won't remain only where you want them. The vines bloom from late spring into summer.

There is a danger when recommending the wisteria *(Wisteria* spp.) clan for the fragrant garden. After all, next to kudzu and honeysuckle, these marching vines will quickly take over most provided trellises and arbors, then set their sights for far horizons. The strength of these grasping vines can actually bend iron pipes. However, if you are fortunate enough to sit beneath a wisteria bower when it's in bloom, you'll never forget the experience.

Wisteria floribunda is the Japanese species with a number of cultivars now available. 'Ivory Towers' has long racemes of pure white blossoms.

Wisteria sinensis, the Chinese wisteria, blooms before the foliage appears.

Wisteria venusta is our American species.

Because of the meandering habits of wisterias, it's best to grow this vine under the watchful eye of volunteers who will promise to trim every tendril as it advances toward other trees and houses. You may want to grow them in containers, where the control is far greater and the vines can be trimmed as a small tree or kept to one trellis. Provide full sun except in the Deep South, where some afternoon shade is appreciated. They are not fussy as to soil type, but they do want good drainage. If your vine doesn't produce flowers, it's either due to a rooted cutting, which will never flower, or to an excess of nitrogen. For the first problem check your supplier; for the second, use a 0-10-10 formula during the growing season.

Chapter 8
Water Gardens

A surprising number of plants for a water garden are fragrant. A few years ago, when I decided to install a water garden of my own, I assumed I'd have to excavate and, in addition, hire somebody to lay concrete forms, plus all the extra fuss that goes with such a venture. But I had not figured on some of the better aspects of plastic.

By using PVC or rubberized sheeting, a material now available from most garden centers, your garden can include a pond of decent size, all accomplished for a very reasonable price. You need only allocate a weekend to dig the hole and do the necessary preparations. If you lack the time for such a pool, you can excavate a small hole and install one of the many free-form fiberglass jobs. For a very small garden, you could use a plastic tub full of water or even half a whisky keg.

Placing the Pond

Even with today's relatively carefree building products, a backyard pond is a major decision, so you should plan before you choose a site. First and foremost is light.

'Wood's White Knight' is a four-star fragrant water lily with its vanilla white petals surrounding lemon-tipped stamens.

Flowering plants in general and water lilies in particular need some sunlight every day in order to blossom. Also, you must have a nearby supply of water. Finally, if the pond is large, local zoning rules should be consulted; many municipalities get touchy about open expanses of water that are easily approached by unattended children.

Location. The spot I chose for my first water garden was a level area that received sunlight from late morning on. It was also close to the terrace, so we could comfortably sit and watch the water, its reflections, and often on a quiet afternoon,

The crushed leaves of the sweet flag (Acorus calamus 'Variegatus') impart a sweet odor and were once used to provide fragrance for hair tonics and pomades.

smell the flowers without leaving our chairs. We installed an electric outlet nearby for outdoor lights for the evening and a pump for filtering the water if I ever decided on goldfish.

Construction. Next I consulted the catalogs to see what size of vinyl liner was available. I found that a 10-by-10-foot liner of extra thick (20 mil.) plastic would make a pool just under 6 by 6 feet and about 18 inches deep. A simple rule of thumb for figuring how much liner to buy: add to your maximum width twice the depth plus 2 feet to allow a 1-foot overlap on all sides. Do the same for the length. I chose battleship gray as the color, but now I would choose black. Unless you are a Hollywood starlet, stay away from turquoise or blue liners.

To make the pool, first dig a hole about 18 inches deep. If you plan on a large pool, use a garden hose to lay out the shape. Find or borrow a line-level to make sure your excavation is on the level; now is the time to be careful. Remove all the rocks, pebbles, or other debris. Next put a $1/2$-inch layer of sand on the bottom and work sand up the sides to fill any holes left by removing stones. If you have especially rocky soil — like we always do — spread a layer of .0002-inch commercial building polyethylene over the sand before you lay down the liner.

Drape the liner into the hole, placing bricks or stones on the sides to hold it in place. Now start filling with tap water using your garden hose. After the pool is full, trim the liner to a 6-inch overhang and cover it with a layer of fieldstones or pieces of slate. If you want a formal look, you could lay stone paving on a bed of mortar.

If you intend to add fish to your pool, let the water settle for a week or so before they join the swim. Use a siphon to empty the pool as needed.

Planting Out. Instead of throwing soil directly into the pool, put all the water lilies and other fragrant plants into individual pots. A good soil mix for all is three parts of good topsoil — and in this case a heavy clay soil is fine — and one part of well-rotted or composted cow manure. Cover the soil after planting with a 1-inch layer of clean gravel to prevent the soil from riling up the water.

Keep control over the number of plants in your pool. It will only hold so much and stay in a healthy state. A 6-by-6-foot pool has a surface area of 36 square feet and will hold only three or four small to medium water lilies and one or two other water plants.

In the North you can treat tropical water lilies as annuals and replace them every season. You can also put them in a greenhouse or a cool (but not freezing) area for the winter. In the South, where winters are Zone 9 and above and temperatures rarely fall below 30°F, they can be left out year-round.

FRAGRANT PLANTS FOR THE WATER GARDEN

The following plants are all fragrant in bloom; a few of the tropical water lilies are fragrant only at night.

Sweet flags *(Acorus calamus),* hardy perennials, enjoy full sun and need a 6-inch depth of water to succeed. The flowers appear on the edges of mature leaves and unless you know, you would never take them as flowers at all. But the leaves and the roots have a very sweet smell when crushed, like honey and cinnamon, and are the source of the drug calamus; they were once primary ingredients in men's hair tonics. *A. calamus* 'Variegatus' is a form with variegated leaves.

Cape pondweed, or water hawthorn *(Aponogeton distachyos),* is a native of the Cape of Good Hope. It's an aquatic that does well in a tub or small garden pond but is not hardy below 20°F or Zone 9. The lance-shaped leaves lie flat on the water, and the waxy white flowers smell of vanilla. There is a rare cultivar called 'Giganteus' with larger flowers.

I hesitate to mention *Houtuynia cordata* because many people think it a rank invader. That said, this plant does well in a few inches of water or in wet soil at the edge of a pond, bearing white begonia-like flowers above heart-shaped blue-green leaves. The plant smells of citrus, but some people feel that it is very strong and disagreeable.

Cowslips *(Primula* spp.) are harbingers of spring and the following species do very well in the moist area around a pond, a place where the soil never completely dries out. All these flowers have a very rich and sweet fragrance. They are all hardy perennials from Zone 5 and south.

The giant cowslip *(Primula florindae)* bears pale yellow, bell-shaped flowers in drooping clusters, usually around midsummer's eve. The Himalayan cowslip

Houtuynia cordata *is a marsh plant. Its foliage bears the scent of the Seville orange — pungent yet refreshing. 'Chameleon' has bright green leaves with red and yellow variegations and is the best choice for gardens.*

The original cowslip Primula veris *blooms early in the spring with a soft fragrance. It makes a fine cut flower that will bring the scent of spring indoors.*

(P. sikkimensis) also bears pale yellow pendent flowers in midsummer. *Primula vialii* sports flowers of a lovely lavender blue. The common English primrose *(P. vulgaris)* has yellow flowers with a deeper yellow center and blooms in early spring.

Lizard's tail *(Saururus cernuus)* is an aggressive hardy perennial that spreads, although it can be easily uprooted if it gets out of hand. This is a charming plant that dotes on the mucky verges of ponds and small streams. The dense, terminal spikes of fragrant white flowers are borne on 2- to 4-foot stems and have a delicious smell of vanilla.

WATER LILIES

All agree that water lilies are the stars of the water world. The hardy lilies will bloom as soon as summer air temperatures reach and remain at 70°F and the water hits 60°F. The tropicals must have several weeks of daytime temperatures in the 80s.

Hardy Water Lilies

Hardy water lilies will do well from USDA Zones 3 up to 11. In northern ponds these lilies die down with the frosts of fall and then return each spring, the leaves appearing well before the flowers. Plants require still water and need 6 to 18 inches of water above the roots.

The native hardy and fragrant water lily *(Nymphaea odorata)* bears lovely white or pink double blossoms up to 4 inches across and, unlike most of the cultivars mentioned below, is considered a miniature by most aquatic experts. This means that a plant can be grown in a 6-inch flowerpot submerged in a small pool. A mature plant needs at least a foot of water above the submerged pot so the leaves can float on the water's surface. Although it's hardy throughout the United States, it must be kept from freezing in ice; therefore, if the water in your pond does freeze to the bottom, store this lily, pot and all, in a cool place and keep the soil moist. As long as water above doesn't freeze, zones are unimportant.

Each of the following water lily cultivars is fragrant with the flowers generally floating on the water's surface. The blossoms open around 9:00 in the morning and close in midafternoon. They often stay closed on cloudy or rainy days. The spread of the plant tells you the size of tub, pool, or pond needed for required growth.

'Arc en Ciel'; 5-inch-wide pastel pink flowers streaked with pinks, creams, and bronze tints stand above olive green leaves. The spread is 9 to 18 square feet.

'Charlene Strawn'; 5-inch-wide yellow flowers are surrounded by mottled green leaves. They bloom with as little as three hours of direct sun. The spread is 6 to 12 square feet.

'Marliacea Carnea'; 4- to 5-inch pale pink flowers have bright green leaves, blooming with as little as three hours of direct sun. The spread is 6 to 12 square feet.

'Masaniello'; 4- to 5-inch pale pink flowers with white outer petals above bright green leaves. The spread is 6 to 12 square feet.

'Rosy Morn'; 6- to 7-inch tulip-shaped flowers with deep pink inner petals and pale pink outside. Stand above purplish leaves that mature to green. The spread is 6 to 12 square feet.

Tropical Water Lilies (*Nymphaea* spp.)

Tropical water lilies bloom year-round in Zones 10 and 11. Unfortunately, everywhere else they are killed by freezing temperatures that last over any length of time. Tropicals must be kept in warm water and must not be planted outside until water temperatures are 70°F or above.

Day-blooming Fragrant Tropical Water Lilies

Just like the hardy day-blooming water lilies, the tropicals open around 9:00 A.M. and close in midafternoon. Many of the day-blooming cultivars are called viviparous, which means they produce little plantlets at the edges. These plantlets are easily detached, pressed into a pan of soil that is covered with a few inches of water, and will soon root and form new flowering plants. The following cultivars are especially fragrant.

'Afterglow'; 6- to 8-inch flowers with yellow to orange petals are surrounded by green leaves. The spread is 9 to 18 square feet.

'Aviator Pring'; 5- to 7-inch flowers with deep yellow petals are held well above the water and green leaves. The spread is 9 to 18 square feet.

'Blue Beauty'; 5- to 6-inch lilac blue flowers with yellow centers. New leaves are blotched with purple-brown and mature to green. The spread is 9 to 18 square feet.

'White Delight'; 7- to 9-inch white flowers with yellow centers are surrounded by new leaves that are mottled with brownish purple, maturing to green. The spread is 9 to 18 square feet.

Night-fragrant Tropical Water Lilies

Night-fragrant lilies do best with six hours of sun or more each day; however, because their plant histories can cope with overhanging vegetation, they will flower with as little as three hours of direct sun.

'Charlene Strawn' is a fragrant, hardy water lily that produces yellow flowers.
They bloom with as little as three hours of direct sun a day.

'Charles Thomas', a lotus of rare beauty, is well suited to growing in a container.

'Emily Grant Hutchings'; 5- to 7-inch pink blossoms stand next to bronze-green leaves with slightly ruffled edges. The spread is 9 to 18 square feet.

'H. C. Haarstick'; 5- to 7-inch rose red flowers with showy orange-red stamens at the center. The deep green leaves are large. The spread is 9 to 18 square feet.

'Wood's White Knight'; 5- to 7-inch pure white blossoms with deep yellow anthers at the center, standing above rich green leaves. The spread is 9 to 18 feet.

The Victoria Water Lily

The great Victorian water lily *(Victoria amazonica)* is not for faint hearts or small ponds, but if you do have the space, this is one spectacular flower. The blossoms, which measure from 8 to 15 inches across, open at dusk and remain open all night. They close partly about 10:30 A.M. and open again at nightfall. As it first expands, the flower is a pure creamy white that gradually changes, as it grows older, to pink, and then to a deep purplish red on the second night.

The best thing about this water lily is the nighttime fragrance, a sweet odor of pineapple with a dash of apples and peaches thrown in for good measure. The fragrance will drift across the water's surface and throughout any nearby garden, and at times, like any perfume, can become almost overpowering.

In order to grow this phenomenal flower you must have a pond at least 2 feet deep and no less than 15 or 20 feet across, and the water temperature must be 70°F.

Lotuses

The lotus *(Nelumbo nucifera)* is a grandiose flower. Its blossoms exude a rich, sweet fragrance and stand well above the leaves on stout stems. Colors include white, rose, pink, yellow, and red. Plants bloom for six to eight weeks in mid-summer, opening early in the morning and closing for the afternoon. The leaves are also fascinating because they repel most liquids; any water that falls on their surface immediately balls up like a drop of mercury and quickly rolls to the edge of the leaf. The cup-shaped seed pods have been used in decorative arrangements for centuries.

Tubers are placed in a tub 20 inches in diameter or larger and need 2 to 4 inches of water above the soil and at least six hours of sun a day. Lotuses are hardy perennials (Zone 4 and above) in most of the United States, but they must have a few weeks of temperatures in the 90s in order to promote bloom. Hence they do not do well in areas with cool summers.

Most lotuses need space, but the following tubers are especially suited to small ponds.

'Alba Grandiflora' has 6- to 8-inch wide flowers of pure white on stems that rise 4 to 5 feet above the water's surface.

'Charles Thomas' bears blooms of lavender-pink, 5 to 7 inches wide. The flowers top 3- to 4-foot stems and are well suited for containers and small pools.

'Momo Botan' displays double rose-pink flowers up to 6 inches across on 2- to 4-foot stems. This is a smaller lotus and perfectly proportioned for a small tub or half a whiskey barrel.

'Mrs. Perry D. Slocum' combines a rich fragrance with deep rose-pink petals on a 7- to 8-inch flower, and the petals change with age to a creamy yellow. They stand above the water on 4- to 5-foot stems.

CHAPTER 9
THE SCENTED GARDEN AT NIGHT

Even though I grew up in the 1950s, lived in Greenwich Village in the 1960s, went to Woodstock in 1969, and have watched moths flocking to night-blooming flowers for years, the last thing I ever thought of when dealing with night-scented flowers was the concept of sex. It was Norman Taylor (that staid practitioner of very traditional tomes) who suggested in his 1953 book *Fragrance in the Garden* that before planning a night garden devoted to fragrance, "No one . . . can escape the implications of an atmosphere redolent with the fragrance of sex." He urged his readers to consider whether their night gardens of fragrance should "reflect the mature scents of the middle-aged" or whether they should be "a thing of haunting beauty, sex-charged with the mystery of night and perfumed with intoxicating fragrance."

The peacock orchid (Acidanthera bicolor) *is a member of the iris family, originally from Ethiopia and available from most bulb suppliers. It is a beautiful and intensely fragrant flower, smelling of sweet violets.*

FLOWERS FOR THE NIGHT

The following are plants for the evening garden which produce their most profound fragrances at dusk or even later in the evening. Some are tropical and must be treated as annuals in a garden where temperatures fall below freezing. Others, like flowering tobaccos, four-o'clocks, annual daturas, moonflowers, evening stock, blazing stars, and *Zaluzianskya capens,* are true annuals or treated as annual plants and are described in the chapter 4.

Two Tender Bulbs

The peacock orchid *(Acidanthera bicolor)* is a member of the iris family from Ethiopia and, as such, is very tender. The sword-shaped leaves arise from corms that produce about six flowers atop 18-inch stalks. The blossoms are creamy white, about 3 inches across, and have a rich chocolate-maroon center. At dusk they begin to produce a sweet scent reminiscent of violets. They need a nighttime temperature no lower than 50°F and will usually bloom in late July from a mid-April planting. After the orchids flower, allow the foliage to die back, then let the corms dry, brush the loose dirt away, and store them over the winter in a cool dry place.

Perfumed fairy lilies *(Chlidanthus fragrans)* belong to a genus of bulbous plants from the Andes of Peru, but only *C. fragrans* is in general cultivation. Three or four yellow funnel-shaped flowers about 4 inches long are carried in clusters on stems about 1 foot high. At night they smell like lilies, and they can be left in the garden if the ground never freezes.

Hardy Perennials

The night-blooming daylily *(Hemerocallis citrina),* a plant that is its own oxymoron, was discovered in central China, specifically the Shensi Province, in 1890 by a Catholic missionary. In 1987 this botanical curiosity was named and the hybridizing circus immediately began. Every daylily breeder in Europe and America was looking for the genetic secret to produce a daylily that would bloom for two days, and *H. citrina* was supposed to hold the secret. Well, it has been a hundred years and a two-day blooming daylily still hasn't been produced!

For the fragrant garden at night, however, this daylily has yet to be bettered. The plant has arching leaves up to 40 inches long, which are rippled along the

Like the lemom lily, the night-blooming daylily (Hemerocallis citrina) *bears the delightful fragrance of lemons, particularly on warm summer nights.*

The true evening primroses are at their best in the late afternoon, when their sweetly scented flowers begin to open. One of the most fragrant is the American biennial Oenothera biennis, *a plant that is at its best in the garden border.*

edges and attractive in their own right. Most important, the narrow flowers open in late afternoon and stay open all night, finally starting to decay about noon of the following day (earlier if the day is excessively warm). The three lemon yellow sepals have streaks of green on their back; the tips are each stained with a blot of purplish brown; and the three petals are pale yellow. The blossoms are sweetly fragrant, and plants bloom for at least three weeks.

There are a number of other fragrant daylilies available. 'Hyperion' has been around since 1925 and remains one of the best cultivars, not only for its form and color but also its light, sweet fragrance. 'Ida Miles' has been around for about as long and is even sweeter. 'Zarahelma' is another nocturnal daylily with pink-lavender flowers, and again is sweetly fragrant.

Care is easy: simply provide a reasonably good soil, full sun in the North and partial shade in the South, and water the plants during long periods of drought.

Dame's rocket *(Hesperis matronalis)* has other common names, such as sweet rocket and rogue's gilliflower. Dozens of half-inch flowers arranged in showy but loose terminal racemes present colors of white, lilac, or purple. Most gardeners describe these flowers as being "deliciously fragrant," especially in the evening, and this is no exaggeration. If you have a first-floor room where people gather, plant dame's rocket under the window. According to Louise Beebe Wilder, who was no slouch when it came to fragrant plants, this flower has the advantage over many other night-scented plants because it doesn't lose its looks or fragrance by day. Deadhead spent blossoms for a second period of bloom. Every few years raise new plants from seed, as older roots get woody and eventually die.

The evening primrose *(Oenothera biennis)* is a true biennial, the seedlings forming rosettes of ground-hugging leaves the first year and holding off bloom until late spring and summer of the second year. But they are worth both the wait and the effort. This species was introduced to gardens in the 18th century as a root vegetable called yellow lamb's lettuce or German rampion. Today it's a star at health-food markets.

While plants that are seen growing in fields and at the edge of roads are small, when sited in good soil, they often reach a height of 5 feet. Before the evening sky turns dark purple, the fresh buds on an evening primrose begin to open in slow motion; the process takes 10 to 15 minutes (depending on the temperature). Then they send out a sweet, lemony odor that attracts some of the living stars in evening entertainment: hawkmoths will fly around you to get to the blossoms. Simply provide full sun and a reasonable soil.

'Bouncing Bet' *(Saponaria officinalis)* is a must for scented gardens both day and night. The genus is named for the Latin *sapo,* or soap, because its mucilaginous sap forms a lather in water. In mid to late afternoon, the flowers are extremely sweet and attract daytime moths like the sphinx moth, plus bees, and then more flamboyant moths when the garden is dark. When the blossoms first open, they reveal five outer stamens that shed pollen on moth and bee alike. Next, five inner stamens do the same, but the female stigma has two caps that protect against self-fertilization.

Give these plants full sun in the North and partial shade in the South. There is a fragrant double cultivar with pink flowers on 2-foot stems, called 'Rubra Plena'.

Tropical Beauties

While topical in habit, the flowers described here are not really houseplants, but spectacular perennials that do their best out in the garden and are only brought indoors if your winters are below freezing. I've limited my selection to those that I consider the most delightful.

The sweet bouvardia, *Bouvardia longiflora,* hails from Mexico and Central America. I found my first plant while checking the tropical imports in the fresh flower section. They can summer outside but need average winter temperatures around 50°F (although for short periods they will survive the low 40s). Plants reach a height of about 3 feet, and if set in hanging baskets, they will arch over the edge. The leaves are a glossy, medium green; toward the branch tips a cluster of white waxy flowers will appear, having four petals at the ends of 3-inch tubes. During the day there is no fragrance, but as evening approaches you'll become aware of a perfume that is a blend of honey and jasmine. Plants bloom in late spring, on into summer, and may be cut back (root the cuttings) for a third bloom in midwinter.

The angel's trumpets, or brugmansias, are tropical plants that belong to the nightshade family and for years were lumped in with the daturas. Most of today's references use the term *Datura* (which see) for those species that are either annu-

Although the daturas have been described as pantropic weeds, the flowers of many are sweetly fragrant and beautiful. Brugmansia suaveolens, *pictured here, originated in South America.*

als or short-lived perennials and *Brugmansia* for the true perennials. Although flowers are open during the day, as evening approaches the blossoms actually swell a bit and produce a heady scent that quickly wafts its way through greenhouse or garden.

These shrubs or small trees produce truly spectacular flowers — nodding, bell-like blossoms that often reach a length of 10 inches. In a tropical garden or the atmosphere of a heated greenhouse, plants can reach a height of 10 feet — but with pruning you can keep them within bounds. Provide evenly moist, well-

composted soil in a spot with as much sun as possible. Never let temperatures fall much below 60°F or growth and flowering is slowed. These plants are very heavy feeders; for continued bloom through the summer, use a liquid fertilizer at least once every three weeks.

There are many different kinds of shrubs available, and the following are among the most impressive. In containers, they all reach a height of between 3 and 6 feet. *Brugmansia* × *candida* 'Double White' will bloom throughout the garden year with startlingly beautiful double blossoms of a trumpet within a trumpet; *B.* × *insignis* 'Pink' bears 9-inch-long salmon pink bells on 6-foot plants;

The perennial daturas (Brugmansia × insignis *'Pink')* *will overwinter in a warm garage, bursting forth with large pendent flowers when summer heats up.*

B. suaveolens is the old-fashioned angel's trumpet producing large white bells throughout the summer; *B. suaveolens* 'Variegata' produces pure white bells that hang over very attractive variegated foliage and is best for small gardens because it reaches a height of only 4 feet.

Rondeletia leucophylla is a tropical shrub that was first imported from Panama and Cuba in 1836. The rose red flowers have a yellow eye, grow in terminal cluster, and are long thin tubes that flare out into five lobes. There is little if any fragrance during the day, but they produce a sweet odor redolent of honey when the sun sets. In containers, plants reach a height of 1 to 3 feet.

CHAPTER 10
FRAGRANT HOUSEPLANTS

Not everybody has a backyard suited to gardening, nor do we all want to spend the time and energy necessary to provide and maintain an outdoor garden. For those gardeners with limited space or time, the following plants are especially suited for the indoor environment, doing well in pots and in the lower light levels found in most homes, even those with very clean windows.

When containerized, the cruel plant *(Araujia sericofera)* is a somewhat constrained vine usually remaining about 3 feet long. When growing on an outside garden wall (only where average temperatures are above 50°F), the vines go 10 feet or more. The summer-blooming flowers are white or pale pink and about an inch wide. The common name is apt and refers to moths flocking to the very sweet blossoms, getting trapped by the sticky pollen, and fluttering all night long until the early morning sun dries the pollen and most of the insects fly away. Because cruel plants belong to the milkweed family, after the flowers fade and turn to seed, large pear-shaped pods break open and reveal a mass of silky threads, allowing the seeds to eventually fly away on the summer air.

The golden chalice vine (Solandra maxima) *produces large fragrant blossoms that turn to gold with age. In the North, it must be brought indoors for the winter.*

The Arabian coffee plant *(Coffea arabica)* is the major source of commercial coffee and the principal coffee-producing species grown in Latin American. But you can have your own Juan Valdez favorite in your garden room or sunporch as long as you keep the temperatures above 55°F and have plenty of bright light. In containers, coffee grows up to 5 or 6 feet, but with good environmental care can grow as tall as 10 feet. Branches are decked with shiny green leaves. In late spring and early summer, clusters of fragrant white starry flowers actually produce pulpy red berries, each containing the two seeds or "beans" that are roasted for coffee. The fruits do take several months to ripen. Keep soil evenly moist and set the plant in filtered sun.

Persian violets *(Exacum affine),* sometimes called Arabian gentians or blue Lizzies, are small tropical perennials usually grown as biennials. The plants are about 6 inches high and are covered with stalked waxy leaves and tiny starlike, bluish-lilac flowers, with an eye formed by a prominent yellow stamen. The blossoms are usually a half-inch wide and sweetly fragrant. For August bloom, start seeds in March. Plants can be grown in pots as greenhouse perennials repeatedly, flowering from June to midfall. Persian violets want warm surroundings, shaded sun, and evenly moist soil.

The Amazon lily *(Eucharis grandiflora)* is a stunning houseplant. Fragrant 2-inch-wide nodding blossoms of pure white are often used by florists in bridal bouquets and make excellent cut flowers. The attractive leaves are broadly ovate on long stalks and evergreen. Because these plants are evergreen, they can be brought into flower at any time of the year. After each flowering period is over, withhold watering for about a month to give the bulbs a short rest. Don't let the leaves wilt. Then resume watering, and new flowers will appear. By alternating two pots of bulbs you will always have these fragrant flowers at hand. Use a good potting soil, place three to six bulbs in a 6-inch pot, and provide warm temperatures (65°F) with filtered sun in the summer and full sun in the winter.

The Cape jasmine is a gardenia *(Gardenia jasminoides)* of great beauty with a fragrance to match. The cultivar 'Prostrata', a dwarf variety, has shiny leaves, a compact growth habit, and small waxy-petaled gardenias throughout the year, peaking from spring into summer. Provide full sun in winter, partial sun in summer, and a minimum temperature of 60°F.

The night gladiolus *(Gladiolus tristis)* grows wild in South Africa, often next to ditches or on the borders of swamps. The creamy yellow flowers, intensely fragrant with a spicy-sweet perfume, rise above unusual leaves that when cut in a cross-section look just like a pinwheel. The frost-tender corms are small. Allow them to dry completely after the leaves die back, then let corms rest about three months before bringing back into growth.

Wax plants (*Hoya* spp.) have been houseplant favorites since the Victorian era. They are exceptional when grown in pots and have a great tolerance to gardeners who ignore them for weeks on end. The most popular members of the clan are *H. carnosa* and *H. bella*. When they bloom, clusters of 12 to 15 perfect star-shaped flowers, each more fragrant than the next and each on a slim stem, open like a living fireworks display. The blossoms look as though they were carved from wax. Then, too, almost every flower will produce a crystal drop of nectar that is incredibly sweet. The smell of warm mocha java is produced by *H. coronaria; H. odorata* smells of citrus in general and lemons in particular; *H. polyneura,* or the fishtail hoya, produces fragrant gems of pure white, each flower boasting a blush-pink center. They prefer a good houseplant soil, evenly moist, but will survive a lack of water for weeks. A great pot is a wire-mesh basket; line it with a sheet of sphagnum moss.

Winter jasmine *(Jasminum polyanthum)* usually provides its masses of fragrant snow-white flowers in the dead of winter. This is a great basket plant, keeping to a height and width of about 3 feet in a container. The minimum temperature is 35°F, with 60°F the average, but to bloom, there has to be a spell of days with temperatures below 60°F.

Jasminum molle hails from Australia, producing sweetly scented flowers in late summer and fall. When grown in containers, the vines reach lengths of 3 feet and need a minimum temperature of 50°F.

Poet's jasmine *(Jasminum officinale grandiflorum),* sometimes called French perfume jasmine, has fragrant double white flowers that halt their display only during late winter. In containers, the general length of the vines remains within the 3-foot range. Provide full sun and a minimum temperature of 45°F.

Jasminum sambac, 'Grand Duke of Tuscany', produces thick fully double white blooms on the stem tips. Unlike the jasmine vines, this is a bush type. In Southeast Asia, a perfumed drink is made by soaking the flowers overnight in water. Provide full sun and minimum temperatures of 60°F.

African gardenia *(Mitriostigma axillare)*, a relative of the gardenia family, offers both bloom and fragrance throughout the year. The dense clusters of pure white flowers stand out from dark green foliage. In pots, these plants stand about 2 feet high, need full sun in winter and partial shade in summer, and minimum temperatures of 55°F.

In bloom, orange jasmine *(Murraya paniculata)* produces the scent of orange blossoms, usually throughout the year; when the plant isn't in bloom, it's in bud. Provide full sun and a minimum temperature of 45°F.

The chalice vine or cup-of-gold *(Solandra guttata)* comes from Mexico and the West Indies. This quick-growing woody climber bears large, oval, thick, shiny leaves. The 10-inch flowers are shaped like goblets, the buds being protected by a green calyx at the base. Blossoms begin as a greenish white, turn to a creamy yellow as they open, and finally to a golden yellow before they fall. The petals are delicately traced with purple. Their fragrance reminds me of fresh coconut. Although the vines rarely climb more than 30 feet, the aerial roots require strong support. Sandy loam is best for a growing medium.

Madagascar jasmine *(Stephanotis floribunda)* is a tropical climber with thick, leathery, glossy, dark green leaves on stems that bloom in the winter months, producing clusters of lovely white waxy trumpet-shaped flowers that flare out to five pointed lobes. This is another flower often used for wedding bouquets. Provide full sun and keep the minimum temperature around 60°F. The vines bloom in spring and summer.

Known as the Confederate jasmine
(for the Confederate States of Malaysia),
Trachelospermum jasminoides *bears fragrant*
white star-shaped blooms in early spring.

The fragrant snowball (Viburnum × carcephalum) *bears large clusters of sweetly fragrant blossoms that are often as wide as 6 inches across.*

HARDINESS ZONE MAP

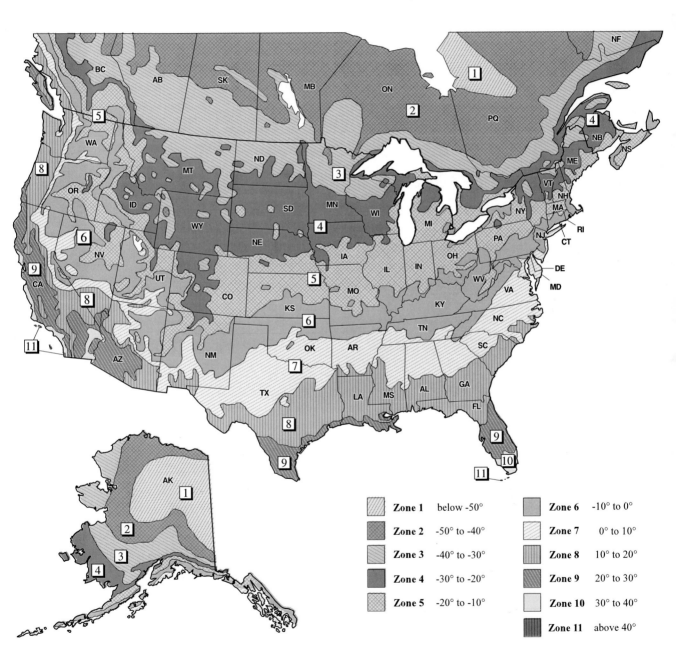

Zone 1	below -50°	**Zone 6**	-10° to 0°
Zone 2	-50° to -40°	**Zone 7**	0° to 10°
Zone 3	-40° to -30°	**Zone 8**	10° to 20°
Zone 4	-30° to -20°	**Zone 9**	20° to 30°
Zone 5	-20° to -10°	**Zone 10**	30° to 40°
		Zone 11	above 40°

PHOTO CREDITS

Rita Buchanan: 105

Derek Fell: 18, 25, 27, 33, 52, 66, 71, 74, 79, 84, 92, back cover

Lilypons Water Gardens: iii, 86, 95, 96

Peter Loewer: vi–1, 29, 43, 46, 67, 72, 98, 101, 106–7, 108

Charles Mann: 22, 41, 42, 61

Tovah Martin: 2

Rick Mastelli: 7, 49, 51, 56, 64

Elvin McDonald: 30

Jerry Pavia: 8, 10, 26, 31, 34, 38, 44, 47, 50, 68, 76, 78, 80, 81, 83, 88, 91, 112, 114

Linda Yang: 54

INDEX

Titles available in the Taylor's Weekend Gardening Guides series:

Organic Pest and Disease Control
Safe and Easy Lawn Care
Window Boxes
Attracting Birds and Butterflies
Water Gardens
Easy, Practical Pruning
The Winter Garden
Backyard Building Projects
Indoor Gardens
Plants for Problem Places
Soil and Composting
Kitchen Gardens
Garden Paths
Easy Plant Propagation
Small Gardens
Fragrant Gardens
Topiaries and Espaliers

At your bookstore or by calling 1-800-225-3362